3-8-60

HARVARD–YENCHING INSTITUTE
MONOGRAPH SERIES
VOLUME XII

Money and Credit in China

A SHORT HISTORY

Money and Credit in China

A SHORT HISTORY

BY

Lien-sheng Yang

Associate Professor of Far Eastern Languages
Harvard University

HARVARD UNIVERSITY PRESS
Cambridge, Massachusetts
1952

Distributed in Great Britain by
GEOFFREY CUMBERLEGE
Oxford University Press, London

Library of Congress Catalog Card Number 52–5413
Printed in the United States of America

Foreword 1168841

This volume contains a short history of money and credit in China centering on a study of key terms. Although numerous books and articles have been written on the subject, many of them tend to be uncritical or have become obsolete. Drawing on more recent and authoritative studies, I have attempted this general account. The period covered is from antiquity to the end of the Ch'ing dynasty. Only occasionally does the narration or discussion touch upon the first decades of the Republic.

In the fall term of 1949, I offered a course on Chinese Economic History at Harvard University. As a part of the course work, I drew up a list of about three hundred key terms in the history of money and banking in China. Having lectured on them, I asked the members of the class to do more research work and write reports on certain groups of these terms. Mr. Stanley Leyden wrote on round coins; Mr. Herbert F. Schurmann on silver and paper currency; and Mr. Francis B. Tenny on banking. These reports have proved useful in the writing of this book. I am happy to acknowledge their contribution.

I owe deep gratitude to my friend and colleague, Dr. Douglas S. Paauw, who has kindly read all ten chapters of the book in manuscript form and made several valuable suggestions from the point of view of an economist. In a number of places he has also improved my English. Of course neither Dr. Paauw nor any of the three students mentioned above should be held responsible for any mistakes or shortcomings in this book.

I am grateful to the Harvard Foundation for Advanced Study and Research for a research grant in the academic year 1950–51, whch facilitated the preparation of the volume.

L. S. Y.

Contents

I Historical Survey 1

II Manifold and Miscellaneous Currency 11

III Round Coins from Antiquity to the
End of the Ch'ing Dynasty 20

IV Some General Problems concerning
Round Coins 30

V Gold and Silver 40

VI Paper Money to the End of the
Sung Dynasty 51

VII Paper Money from the Yüan Dynasty
to the End of the Ch'ing Dynasty 62

VIII Traditional Credit Institutions 71

IX Old-style and Modern-style Banks 81

X Loans and Interest Rates 92

Notes 105

Index to Chinese Characters 117

Money and Credit in China

A SHORT HISTORY

I

Historical Survey

1.1 The evolution of money and credit in a society may be construed to be a barometer of the development of private economy and public finance. Economic progress may, for example, be measured by the percentage of the total economy in which money is used. The development of credit is practically indispensable for the growth of commerce and industry on a large scale. A history of money and credit will be concerned with such questions as: What materials were used as money? Who enjoyed the right of coinage and note issue? What taxes were paid in kind and what in money? What was the extent of legal tender? What banking facilities were available? What was the average interest rate? Were the loans used for investment purposes or for consumption expenditure? Definite answers to these questions will throw light on both the history of money and credit and economic history in general. This book will attempt to find answers to these questions.

1.2 In this chapter of historical survey, I shall first discuss the different functions of money in Chinese history, next proceed to problems concerning credit, and finally attempt to offer some interpretation of the whole picture. The period covered is from antiquity to the beginning of the twentieth century. A number of generalizations will be made, which of course are to be understood only as general patterns, without regard to individual variations. Significant details will be given in the body of the book, which is primarily a study of key terms.

1.3 Money has two main functions: that of a medium of exchange and that of a means of payment. These two functions are sometimes considered as one, but a distinction can be made between them by limiting the first to exchange for commodities and the second to other kinds of payment such as payment of taxes. Tracing the history of money in China, I have found it useful to distinguish between them, because they were not developed to the same degree. As a medium of exchange, money in the form of coins and bullion circulated regularly from as early as the fourth and third centuries before Christ. The coins were made of copper, or to be exact bronze, in the shape of knives and spades. In Han times (206 B.C.–220 A.D.) a round coin with a square hole in the middle was the standard medium for ordinary transactions. Remarkably enough, such coins continued in circulation for more than two thousand years, until the end of the Manchu dynasty (1644–1912).

1.4   A standard medium for large transactions, however, proved to be a much more difficult problem. Gold in catties served the purpose fairly well in Han times. In the period of disunion following the fall of the Han empire until about 600, bolts of silk of a standard length and breadth were used as the main medium of exchange in large transactions. This was also true for the first part of the T'ang period (618–906); but gold and silver began to assume importance. Paper money circulated from the eleventh century on; its origin was in a system of drafts in the ninth century. Under the Yüan dynasty (1279–1368), paper currency in different denominations was prescribed the sole medium of exchange while the circulation of copper cash, gold, and silver was stopped by imperial order. Unfortunately, the government paid insufficient attention to reserves supporting these notes. Large amounts of paper money were issued to meet financial deficits with no regard for the value of the money. Malignant inflation was inevitable, and the people lost confidence in paper notes and turned more and more to silver. From about 1400, silver ingots became the main medium in large transactions. These were supplemented from around 1700 on with notes issued by local banks. Thus, so far as a medium of exchange is concerned, China may be said to have had a money economy for about twenty-four centuries. The use of bolts of silk in medieval China (c. 200–600) may seem to indicate a return to barter, but they were actually a medium of exchange for large transactions. Round coins were still used during the greater part of the era. For a short period, these seem to have gone out of use in north China, but remained in circulation in the Yangtse valley continuously.

1.5   The general picture presented above is, of course, subject to modification. Historical and regional divergences did, and still do, exist. In some cases they resulted from natural economic developments and in others from arbitrary decisions made by the government. It has been pointed out that copper cash was the accepted medium of exchange for more than two thousand years. Round coins made of other metals, however, also circulated from time to time. Of these the most important was undoubtedly iron cash, first cast in the Szechwan area at the beginning of the Christian era. Throughout the first millennium its use was alternately abandoned and reinstated and its area of circulation was, on the whole, confined to the Yangtse valley. The Sung dynasty (960–1279) cast more copper and iron coins than the preceding dynasties, but arbitrarily confined the use of iron cash to certain border provinces to prevent the export of copper coins to the north and northwest. Iron coins, however, had little importance in the Ming (1368–1644) and Ch'ing periods except as occasional means of financing extraordinary expenditures.

1.6 In addition to regional and historical differences, it must be added that even in the same place and at the same time, complete uniformity in currency did not exist and exceptions to standard practices were accepted as inevitable. Small and counterfeit coins were found in practically every string of cash entering the market. Silver of different degrees of fineness and varying tael weight made the assay shop a necessity. Foreign traders in nineteenth-century China were particularly annoyed by this chaotic state of the currency.

1.7 In spite of these differences, it remains true that copper cash was a standard for ordinary transactions. For large transactions, gold, silk, paper money, and silver were used as the predominant medium of exchange in four periods. From this survey we may conclude that a medium of exchange evolved early in Chinese history, and existed continuously to the present.

1.8 As for means of payment for occasions other than trade transactions, the story is different. For the greater part of the last two thousand years, tax in kind remained the major form of government revenue, and rent in kind that of a landlord's income. In addition, labor services were required by the government from the people and occasionally by the landlord from his tenants. Salaries of government officials as a rule were only partly determined and paid in terms of money. A private employee would almost certainly receive his wage or salary in money, but, in addition, he would expect his employer to provide him with food and shelter. This was true in the case of journeymen in workshops, clerks in stores, servants in households as well as hired hands on farms. As a prescribed means of tax payment, money assumed significance from about 800 and became predominant from about 1600. Taxation in kind, being collected in terms of many types of commodities in differing measurements, was very complicated. Such collection of taxes only gradually gave way to taxation in terms of money. Two famous tax reforms were instrumental in this change. The Two-tax system introduced in 780 made many taxes payable in copper cash; the Single-whip system of the sixteenth century prescribed collections in silver. The implementation of the second reform in the following centuries made it possible for China to use simple monetary calculations in public finance.

1.9 In addition to the primary functions of money discussed above, money has two additional functions: as a standard of value and as a store of value. The two latter functions are corollary to the former, and consequently subsidiary. Since they will not be treated at length in the body of the book, these subsidiary functions are discussed in this chapter in some detail.

1.10 In Chinese history, coins and bullion have served both purposes. The practice of reckoning one's property in terms of money began in ancient times. For instance, from references of the second century B.C., we learn that an average household owned property valued at ten catties of gold, or the equivalent of 100,000 cash. A rich moneylender might have had ten times this amount (1,000,000 cash), which, loaned out at the prevailing 20 per cent interest rate, would bring him an annual income of 200,000 cash. Paper money was issued in terms of copper cash or silver bullion, and used the same unit of account as the metallic currency. The tael of silver was such a popular unit of value that it remained in commercial use even after the adoption of the silver dollar as the official unit of the Republic. It was not until 1933 that businessmen were ordered to give up the use of the tael as their accounting unit. This change is known as *fei-liang kai-yüan,* "abolition of the tael and change to the dollar."

1.11 Money, as indicated by its synonym currency, is intended for circulation; it should not remain idle. This was clearly recognized in the case of copper coins. For instance, when there was a serious shortage of cash in the ninth century, imperial decrees were issued prohibiting the hoarding of copper coins above a specified number of strings. The situation was different, however, with reference to precious metals. Prior to the modern era of Chinese history, which began in the nineteenth century, the hoarding of large sums of gold and silver was a common practice. In this matter the emperor, the imperial princes, and top-ranking officials were naturally in the lead. The records indicate that when Imperial Prince Hsiao of Liang, of the Han dynasty, died in 144 B.C., he had accumulated 400,000 catties of gold in his treasury. When the usurper-emperor Wang Mang was destroyed in 23 A.D., he left in his palaces 600,000 catties of gold.

1.12 One of the richest individuals in Chinese history was the notorious minister Ho Shên, of the Ch' ing period. Impeached and executed in 1799, he left property which amounted to several tens of million taels of silver. According to an imperial decree which lists his crimes, in addition to money found in his regular treasuries, people discovered over 6,000 taels of gold in a secret treasury, over 26,000 taels of gold hidden in the walls of his house, and over 1,000,000 taels of silver buried in his cellars. In his bedrooms, people found large gold "shoes" (*yüan-pao*), large silver "shoes," and a gold pagoda. Unofficial accounts give different details about his confiscated property, but two sources agree in saying that these large "shoes" of precious metals represented 100,000 taels of gold and the same amount of silver. The total amount of gold and silver thus hoarded in his house must have been considerable.

1.13 Throughout the period of imperial China, it was not only individual members of the ruling classes who held large amounts of gold and silver. It was also the standard practice for the government itself to store up precious metals and other valuables. These accumulations were intended for emergency, because it was inconceivable that a government could live on loans. In the Ch'ing period, even the treasuries of the provincial and district government were ordered to keep large amounts of silver on hand. Deficit financing is an entirely modern idea.

1.14 The story of credit in China may be summarized in one word: underdevelopment. Loans were made typically for short terms and at high rates of interest. This made it difficult to do business with borrowed capital. A man could start a business only when he himself had accumulated enough money to cover the initial investment, and only then could he induce his relatives or friends to join. Farmers as a rule borrowed from season to season, and it has been estimated that less than half of their borrowings were used for productive purposes, the remainder being used for consumption expenditures.

1.15 The practice of lending money at interest can be traced back at least as far as the fourth century before Christ. In Han times professional moneylenders were known as *tzŭ-ch'ien chia,* literally, "interest (making) specialists." Government regulations on usury were proclaimed in this period and sometimes actually enforced. A couple of nobles lost their titles because they charged excessive rates of interest. Regulations governing rates of interest and terms of loans were proclaimed from dynasty to dynasty, but unfortunately they were often ignored.

1.16 Since loans were generally made for consumption purposes, it was considered shameful to resort to borrowing. As a matter of fact, there were no regular credit institutions to which a member of the upper classes could turn without disgracing himself. Pawnshops were supposed to serve only the very poor. When a person of high social standing had to use the facilities of a pawnshop it was customary for him to send a servant to carry out the transaction, and even the servant would make efforts to conceal his identity. Actually the same face-saving psychology was found among poor people. An inexperienced borrower would turn to the first pawnshop or moneylender and transact his business as quickly as possible. Failing to engage in higgling and comparison of terms, he became an easy victim of usury.

1.17 Although channels for obtaining loans were few for the needy, credit sales to respectable customers was a general practice among shopkeepers. In theory, credit was extended not because the customer might be short of cash but as a matter of convenience. It was considered a matter of prestige to be able to buy on credit. Like other debts, these credit sales were settled three times a year, on New Year's Eve and at two festivals in the fifth and eighth months of the year. Sales on credit between the wholesaler and the retailer, however, were comparativly rare because they involved more risk. On the whole, credit was extended as a recognition of social status rather than as a means of expanding business.

1.18 The earliest known credit institution was the pawnshop, which first appeared in Buddhist monasteries in about the fifth century. From T'ang times on, pawnshops were also operated by the laity. Nevertheless monastic pawnshops continued to be popular as late as the fourteenth century. Emperors of the Yüan dynasty issued many decrees exempting Buddhist and Taoist monasteries from paying taxes on their pawnshops. In Ming and Ch'ing times pawnshops operated by laymen developed so much that most people forgot that the institution was once confined to monasteries. One or more pawnshops would be found in every city and town and in many villages. The government laid down detailed regulations on the rate of interest which might be charged and the period allowed for redemption. These apparently were better observed than the rules against usury in general.

1.19 Another important credit institution in traditional China was the coöperative loan society. It was a temporary organization of friends or relatives to finance one of its members in particular or all members in turn. Various names were given to such coöperatives, and they seem to have existed in every province of China. The rate of interest was determined either by agreements or, more frequently, by bidding or the drawing of lots. In a few exceptional cases no interest was charged. One advantage of this credit institution was that the rate was usually lower than that required by a moneylender or pawnbroker. Another advantage was that no collateral was required. Instead, one needed a good personal record and family background. The institution, therefore, was used more by the lower middle classes than by the poorest classes.

1.20 Proto-banks existed from the middle of the T'ang dynasty. These were shops dealing with gold, silver, and commodity vouchers issued by the government against monopoly goods like salt and tea. Part of their business was to issue promissory notes and to remit money to distant places. They accepted deposits, but it is not clear whether or not they made loans. In Ming and Ch'ing times banking functions were performed largely by two kinds of business: the gold and silversmiths and the money shops. Ordinary shopkeepers would also receive deposits from customers, sometimes merely as a courtesy but often as usable funds. Public money was also entrusted to wealthy businessmen like salt merchants or pawnbrokers at a reasonable rate of interest.

1.21 From the eighteenth century on, native banks organized by Shansi bankers began to establish a network covering the major cities of the empire. Making profit by remitting money to distant places and by taking deposits and making loans, they were the first banks in China which deserved the name. Native banks organized by people from other places, notably Ningpo, soon developed and competed vigorously with the Shansi banks in South China. In the second half of the nineteenth century modern banks of foreign and native ownership began to function. The result was a gradual lowering of the interest rate in large cities. Towns and villages were only slightly affected.

1.22 A brief survey of the history of money and credit thus reveals the following features: (1) The government made efforts to maintain copper cash as a standard medium for small transactions. A medium for large transactions was sought in gold, silk, paper money, and silver. The government monopolized the issue of paper currency but expressed little interest in the coinage of precious metals. (2) In the field of public finance, the use of coins, metal ingots, and paper notes applied to only a few items of revenue and expenditure. Money economy in China did not go much beyond commercial transactions and failed to dominate the public economy until around 1600. (3) Hoarding of precious metals was a common practice, which undoubtedly contributed to the restriction of economic activities. (4) Lack of banking facilities and the prevalence of short-term loans at high interest rates mark the history of credit in China. Loans were generally used for consumption purposes and not for the creation of capital.

1.23 Explanation of this situation is to be sought in the nature of the Chinese society. In spite of considerable growth of commerce and industry, China has remained primarily an agricultural society. To secure peace and order, the ruling classes sought a balance of economic forces called equalization or stabilization. It was believed that the farmer as the chief producer should receive encouragement and protection. Stabilization of the price of grain became a major concern of the government. The famous Ever-Normal Granary system was merely one device to attain this goal. By collecting tax levies in agricultural produce, the government became the sole giant collector and distributor of grain and silk. This increased tremendously state power to stabilize the prices of such commodities. Incidentally, this meant less business for merchants and less use of money.

1.24 Traditional thought and government policy were generally unfavorable to the merchants. Commerce was considered a secondary occupation for wicked people. Early in Han times merchants were prohibited by law from wearing silk and riding in wagons. In addition, heavy taxes were levied on them. The denial of a high standard of living did not become actually effective; heavy taxation, however, discouraged many a businessman. When the civil service examination system was established in T'ang times, merchants and artisans were classified as irregular groups. Members of their families were excluded from the privilege of taking the general examination, which was the main channel to officialdom. Moreover, since the government exercised monopolistic control over several key commodities like salt and tea, the sphere of activities of private merchants was inevitably restricted.

1.25 Although a large country, China has had only limited resources to support its large population. It was discovered in ancient times that human demand must first be reduced in order to maintain peace in an economy of scarcity. The ruling classes generally attempted to give the ruled a minimum standard of living and tried to persuade them to be contented with it. Minute regulations were laid down for the different social strata, concerning not only matters of living such as shelter, clothes, and vehicles, but also matters of afterlife such as enshrouding, funerals, and sacrifices. The best articles were reserved for imperial use, and leading artisans were called to serve in government workshops. The common folk were supposed to be satisfied with their very limited possessions. To set a good example, certain members of the upper classes also tried to reduce their own wants by imposing self-control.

1.26 On the whole, the ruling classes were successful in making China a contented society, in contrast with the acquisitive nature of Western society which characterized the early growth of capitalism. One reason for this success was that China's neighbors were generally poorer in resources than herself. After reaching a certain limit, Chinese expansion by conquest became subject to the law of diminishing returns. Wars against non-Chinese were more frequently fought for self-defense than for other reasons.

1.27 In a contented society with limited business activities, money was considered to be a necessary evil, and its functions were restricted as far as possible. That is why the Chinese did not find it inconsistent to employ money in commercial transactions while using goods as a means of payment in public finance. The Chinese government did not make any serious attempt to coin precious metals, perhaps because the demand for such a medium of exchange was not strong enough to induce the state to take action. Paper money was taken over from private hands as a state monopoly, apparently both to furnish businessmen with a convenient means of exchange and to derive profit from its issuance. Nevertheless it should be pointed out that the period of paper currency (about 1000 to 1400) witnessed a spectacular growth of commerce and trade, while the period of silver currency which followed was one of slow but steady economic development.

1.28 Loans at high rates of interest and for short terms were the result of insufficient liquid capital. Since loans were generally made for consumption purposes, they added little to the accumulation of capital goods. Moreover, since a small amount could bring considerable income, many people would retire from work as soon as they had saved enough money to provide for them through the remainder of their lives. The combined effect of these factors was a vicious circle of high rates of interest and small accumulations of liquid capital. The main reason was the operation of non-economic forces, since high interest rates would normally encourage large accumulations of capital.

1.29 A similar interpretation may be given to the unequal rates of return in the different fields of traditional investment. Historical references indicate that the rate of return was highest for moneylending, somewhat less for commerce and industry, and lowest on land. Investment in land, however, carried other than economic advantages. For instance, land cannot be stolen or easily destroyed. The landlord was always among the respectable ruling classes. He could also supplement his income by making loans to his tenants, which also would help to retain them on his land. Even businessmen who had made fortunes from shopkeeping, mining, and similar undertakings would consider buying land when they wanted to play a safer game. A combination of commerce or industry and moneylending could be more profitable, but it would be subject to many government controls and restrictions, involve great risks, and carry little prestige.

1.30 The factors checking the progress of commerce and industry in an agricultural society undoubtedly contributed to the economic stagnation of traditional China. The vicious circle between limited capital accumulation and high rates of interest can be broken only when new means of production are introduced to make it more profitable to borrow for productive purposes or when capital from outside becomes available. These new forces in turn would require a uniform and standard medium of exchange and good banking facilities. The history of money and credit thus reveals the traditional pattern in old China, and points to the direction of new developments in the modern world.

II

Manifold and Miscellaneous Currency

2.1 This chapter deals with the manifold currency of ancient China prior to the unification in 221 B.C. and the miscellaneous currency of the subsequent imperial era. The former consists of cowry money, spade coins, knife coins, and certain kinds of commodity money. The latter includes commodity money such as grain and silk and token tablets which supplemented the major currency.

2.2 Like most peoples in the world, the ancient Chinese passed through a period of barter exchange. The primitive trade of China is best described in an appendix to the *Book of Changes* called *Hsi-tz'ŭ*: "Market time was set at noon. The people and the commodities of the world were gathered. Each person traded what he had for what he had not and was satisfied." This passage has been quoted repeatedly from Han times down to the present.

2.3 When certain commodities were found frequently in demand and generally acceptable, they readily acquired the function of a medium of exchange. Thus commodity money was historically the first currency. It tended to be multiple and appear in numerous forms. As a matter of fact, every kind of money used in primitive economies relied heavily upon its intrinsic value as a commodity. This was also true in ancient China.

2.4 The two characters meaning money in Chinese are *huo*, "commodity," and *pi*, "offering, gift," which, put together, make the compound *huo-pi*, a modern technical term for "money, currency." Articles which are referred to as ancient *huo* or *pi* in texts of Han or earlier date include the following items:

1. *chu-yü*, jade and pearls
2. *kuei-pei*, tortoise shells and cowries
3. *ch'üan-ma*, dogs and horses

4. *p'i-pi,* leather
5. *pu-po,* hemp and silk cloth
6. *ku,* grain
7. *chin,* metal

Apparently these objects which were commodities, offerings, or gifts also served occasionally as money.

2.5 Indications are that these various kinds of commodity money could hardly have been used by people of all classes. Ancient texts mention *shang-pi,* "superior money," and *hsia-pi,* "inferior money," and sometimes also *chung-pi,* "intermediate money." Articles like jade, pearl, and gold were superior money and were not expected to be used by the common people. These terms seem to indicate a class distinction in the use of money, a feature found in many cultures.

(*1*) *Cowry Money*

2.6 Early tradition suggests that cowries, or Cypraea shells, were used as money in very ancient China. Although evidence is not conclusive, this seems to have been true in the second half of the second millennium B.C. and the first half of the first millennium B.C.

2.7 There is no doubt that cowries were highly valued by the ancients. Inscriptions on bones and tortoise shells datable to the Shang period (c. 1523–c. 1027 B.C.) and inscriptions on bronze vessels datable to both Shang and the following Early Chou (c. 1027–771 B.C.) periods contain records of grants and gifts of cowries in numbers of *p'êng,* "double strings," in many cases along with other valuables such as land and slaves. In a bronze inscription which appeared probably toward the end of the Early Chou period, we read, "Prince Huan of Ch'ü had this precious vessel *kuei* made for himself, using fourteen double strings of cowries." This obviously indicates the use of cowries as a means of payment.

2.8 To prove that cowries were used as money, scholars often point to the composition of a number of Chinese characters, or written words, which contain the element *pei,* "the cowry," as their "signific" or meaningful root. For instance, characters meaning "to purchase" (*mai*), "to sell" (*mai*), "to store up" (*chu*), "to bestow" (*lai*), and "to treasure" (*pao*) all contain the element *pei,* "the cowry," in their very archaic forms as well as in their later forms. Obviously the relationship between cowries and wealth and commercial transactions in ancient times must have been very close.

2.9 However, this does not mean that the cowry was the only object which performed certain functions of money in ancient China. The

Shih-chi or *Historical Records* written in the first century B.C. says, "When the way of exchange had been opened between agriculturists, artisans, and merchants, then the monetary values of tortoise shells and cowry shells, metals, spades and knives, and hempen and grass cloths arose from it. The origin [of this exchange] was long ago and far away." Apparently the cowry was merely one of several valuables which were used occasionally as money. Actually there was probably no need of a regular medium of exchange, because it is fairly certain that barter transactions remained the predominant form of exchange in Shang and Early Chou times.

2.10　Several plausible reasons can be advanced to explain why cowries were considered valuable by ancient Chinese. The first is obvious, namely, that they can be used as ornaments of personal adornment. The second is that the cowry, particularly its ventral side, may have been connected with superstitions about fecundity. Many ancient specimens actually have their dorsal side filed away, and imitation cowries made from bone, ivory, jade, bronze, and other materials, as a rule represent only the ventral side. A third reason is that sea shells were used as agricultural implements in ancient China. These presumably were larger than the cowry; nevertheless, the practical use of the former may have added something to the value of the latter. If this is true, cowry money may from this point of view be considered similar to the ancient metallic money in the shape of a spade, another agricultural implement.

2.11　According to a Western expert, "The cowries used as money had a hole pierced through the dorsal side of the shell, usually near the small end, in order that they could be strung on cords," whereas all the imitations examined by him "have had two small holes bored in them, evidently for the purpose of sewing them on clothing, or stringing them together so as to make bracelets, necklaces and such like." Since both kinds are capable of being strung on cords or strings, the distinction appears arbitrary. The following explanation of the formulation of a double string is however interesting: "After the cowries were strung the strings were attached to either end of short sticks convenient for carrying in hand." This is illustrated by the archaic form of the character *p'êng,* "double strings," which is a pictograph. Traditions identify a *p'êng* as either two or five cowries. Judging from the pictograph, *p'êng* probably indicated a double string of about five cowries each.

2.12　Certain copper pieces, oval in shape, are believed to be very ancient coins. These coins, known as *i-pi ch'ien* or "ant-nose coins" among numismatists, were probably imitations of cowry money from the period of Warring States (481–221 B.C.). Large quantities of "ant-nose money" have been unearthed in Ku-shih, in southeastern Honan. Many of them bear an inscription resembling an ugly face, and consequently the nickname *kuei-lien ch'ien* or "devil-face money" arose. Authorities have not agreed on the deciphering of this and other inscriptions on "ant-nose money" but agree that they were metallic cowry. The famous dictionary *Shuo-wên chieh-tzŭ* says, "The Ch'in dynasty (221–207 B.C.) abolished the cowry money and put [round] coins into circulation." A reasonable interpretation of this tradition is that the Ch'in abolished the "ant-nose coins," which were imitations of the cowry money, and circulated the round coins. Otherwise the statement would appear puzzling because apparently cowry money did not continue much beyond the Early Chou period (c. 1027–771 B.C.).

2.13   The famous usurper-emperor Wang Mang (9–23 A.D.) was very anxious to revive various practices of antiquity. Among the several kinds of money issued during his short reign were tortoise shell money in four denominations and cowry money in five, to be used along with copper cash, spade money, and gold and silver by weight. This was the only attempt to reintroduce cowries as money, and it failed.

2.14   In the Yunnan province, which borders Burma, however, cowries were used as money as late as Yüan and Ming times. This is mentioned by Marco Polo and various other sources. The names for cowries in this province were *pa-tzŭ* and *hai-pa*. One shell was known as a *chuang* (perhaps *chuang* meaning "adult"), four shells as *shou*, "hand," four *shou* as a *miao*, "sprout," and five *miao*, i.e., eighty shells, as a *so*, "string." This use of cowries was probably influenced by similar practices in India and Burma. After the seventeenth century cowry money in Yunnan began to be replaced by silver and copper.

(2) *Spade Coins and Knife Coins*

2.15   Spade coins or *pu* and knife coins or *tao* are for the most part attributable to a period from the fifth to the third century B.C., and possibly earlier. They are bronze coins of various sizes, about two to eight inches long and about one half to two inches wide. They have been so named by numismatists because they were imitations of these useful tools.

2.16   These coins often bear inscriptions indicating the town, and in some cases the state, where they were minted. By studying these inscriptions and the places where such coins have been unearthed, it is possible to determine their places of origin and areas of circulation. Spade coins have been found largely in the modern provinces of Shensi, Shansi, Honan, and Hopeh, and knife coins primarily in Shantung and Hopeh. A type of knife money known as *Ming-tao* (because it bears the word Ming) is found not only in Shantung and Hopeh but also in southern Manchuria and northern Korea. Ming was probably a town in Hopeh province. Less frequent than place names but still quite common in occurrence are inscriptions indicating the weight of the coins or simply a serial number. A small portion of the coins bears no inscriptions at all.

2.17 Both spade money and knife money include several types. Among the former we may distinguish the "hollow-handle" type (*k'ung-shou pu*), the "poited-foot" type (*chien-tsu pu*), the "square-foot" type (*fang-tsu pu*), and "round-foot" type (*yüan-tsu pu*). Further distinctions can be made in most of these types, depending on whether their "shoulders" are square or round. The "hollow-handle" type, mostly discovered in Honan, was probably the earliest of the spade coins.

2.18 Knife coins are mainly of two types. A thin and light type, including the *Ming-tao* mentioned above, is often found in Hopeh and Honan provinces. A heavy and thick type is found in Shantung and was generally known as *Ch'i-tao*, because the ancient state of Ch'i was located in that province. They bear inscriptions like *Ch'i-tsao-pang ch'ang-fa-huo*, "Everlasting legal money of Ch'i at the establishment of the state," *Ch'i-fa-huo*, "Legal money of Ch'i," and *Chi-mo fa-huo*, "Legal money of Chi-mo," Chi-mo being a town in Ch'i.

2.19 The date of the establishment of Ch'i should be a good clue to the dating of the coin, but unfortunately there were two states called Ch'i in ancient China. Traditional scholars believe that the coin commemorated the founding of the Ch'i state by the Chiang clan in the eleventh century B.C. Consequently they consider the Ch'i knife coins to be earlier than the thinner and lighter type. Some modern scholars, however, tend to identify it with the replacement of the ruling house of Ch'i by the T'ien clan in 402 B.C. They think that the Ch'i coins may have been later than thinner and lighter knife coins like the *Ming-tao* and the *chien-shou tao,* a "pointed-tip" type. One authority asserts that earlier bronze coins contain much more lead. Another argues for the early date of certain types by reason of their closer resemblance to an actual knife, spade, or ploughshare. As yet no general agreement has been reached.

2.20 The inscriptions of Ch'i knives indicate a legal money recognized, if not issued, by the feudal state. This tallies with the term *Wang-tao,* "the King's knives," in the *Mo-tzŭ,* a philosophical work of about the fourth century B.C. The passage reads, "The (weight of the) King's knife does not change but the price of grain does. In a year when prices of grain change, it means a (corresponding) change (in the value) of the knives." This is clearly a recognition of the inverse ratio between the price of commodities and the value of money. When the Han scholar Chia I recommended government monopoly of coinage in 175 B.C., he used in his memorial the expression *fa-ch'ien,* "legal coins," a synonym for *fa-huo.* The year 112 B.C. marked the beginning of imperial monopoly of round coins, a practice continued throughout Chinese imperial history. As legal money of a feudal state, the Ch'i knives marked an earlier government intervention into coinage, which seems formerly to have been the concern of towns or private merchants.

2.21 Spade coins and knife coins went out of use after the unification of China by the Ch'in in 221 B.C. The only attempts to reintroduce such coins were made by Wang Mang. In 7 A.D. he issued "knife" money, called *ch'i-tao* and *ts'o-tao, i.e.,* "carved knives" and "inlaid knives." The former had a circular head like the square hole coin and a body in the shape of a knife; it was valued at five hundred cash. The latter was similar in shape, with the two characters on the coin head inlaid with real gold. It was valued at five thousand cash.

2.22 In 9 A.D. a much more elaborate system was introduced to replace the earlier coins. Five kinds of material (gold, silver, tortoise shells, cowries, copper) were used as currency in as many as twenty-eight denominations. Among these were ten denominations of spade money, valued from one hundred to one thousand cash. The system was found too confusing and abolished in 14 A.D. Spade money called *huo-pu* and round coins called *huo-ch'üan* were then issued as legal currency. The former was equivalent to five of the latter, and the latter, having the weight 5-*shu* (which was standard almost throughout Han times), was worth one cash unit. These coins were gradually abolished at the beginning of the Latter Han dynasty (25–220 A.D.).

(3) Commodity Money in Imperial China

2.23 In commercial transactions, metallic money in the form of gold bullion and copper coins played the predominant role in Han times. In the period of the Six Dynasties following the fall of the Han empire, the leading position of gold and copper passed to such commodity moneys as grain, silk, and hemp cloth. In 221, Emperor Wên of the Wei dynasty abolished the copper coin and ordered the people to use grain and silk as media of exchange. Copper cash was officially restored in 227. The coins however were insufficient, often debased, and circulated only in limited areas. Grain and textiles remained the important forms of currency. The Northern Wei dynasty which ruled north China from 386 to 534 had such a primitive economy that coins did not circulate until 496. The use of copper cash continued in the central and lower Yangtse valley; but in the other parts of south China, grain and silk still performed the function of medium of exchange. In the histories of this period of disunion, we find many examples in which grain, silk, and hemp cloth functioned as media of exchange, means of payment, and standards of value.

2.24 Having a high value and light weight, silk continued to serve as money even in the T'ang period. Although copper cash had recovered its leading position, silk still ranked second and played a more important role than gold and silver. The Japanese scholar Katō Shigeru listed the monetary functions of silk in T'ang times as follows.

(I) In private economy: (1) as bribes concerning public affairs or gifts to procure favor in private relations; (2) as gifts out of courtesy or favor; (3) as donations to temples; (4) as remunerations or tokens of gratitude; (5) as prizes; (6) as traveling expenses; (7) in payment for commodities; (8) as indicators of value; (9) to pay freight charges; (10) as loans; (11) hoarding.

(II) In public economy: (1) taxes; (2) forwarding of local revenues to the central government; (3) tribute to the imperial courts; (4) general state expenses; (5) military expenses.

2.25 Most of the examples cited by Katō, however, belonged to the early part of the T'ang period. Actually, from the eighth century on, silk gradually fell into disfavor as a medium of exchange. In 732, an imperial decree criticized as unreasonable the current practice of insisting on payments in cash and ordered that silk and hemp cloth should be accepted as media of exchange along with copper coins. In 811, a decree ordered that whenever the commodity was valued over ten strings of cash, part of the payment should be made in silk or grain. These imperial decrees however were of little effect. The days of commodity money as a predominant medium of exchange were over.

2.26 In certain backward areas, commodity money continued to exist. For instance, according to a ninth century report, salt and silk were used as money in Szechwan; cinnabar and quicksilver were used as money in Kwangsi, in addition to pieces of cloth and silk. The use of salt as money was noted in several districts in Yunnan and Kweichow as late as the seventeenth century. This, of course, was limited to isolated places.

2.27 Public finance remained the stronghold of commodity money. Taxation in kind was the main source of government revenue from Han to T'ang times. In the year 749, taxation in terms of money formed only 3.9 per cent of the state income. The percentage became higher after the introduction of the two-tax system in 780. Under the Northern Sung dynasty, taxes collected in coin made up 17.6 per cent of the total revenue in 1021, 30.9 per cent in 1049, and 51.6 per cent in 1065. Taxation in money superseded taxation in kind in Southern Sung and Yüan times because of the extensive use of paper currency. Taxation in kind recovered its predominant position under the Ming dynasty but gradually gave way to taxation in silver after the sixteenth century.

(4) Token Tablets

2.28 Small tablets known as *p'ai-tzǔ* or *ch'ou* were used as token money in traditional China. The earliest known *p'ai-tzǔ* were the copper tablets of Hangchow when it was the capital of the Southern Sung dynasty. They were about three inches long and half an inch wide with a round hole near the top to facilitate stringing. On one side were cast the characters *Lin-an-fu hsing-yung*, "to circulate in Lin-an-fu (i.e., Hangchow)." On the other side were words like *chun-wu-pai-wên-shêng*, "The equivalent of 500 cash short-reckoning (i.e., 77 for each string of 100)." Others were for 300 and 100 (and perhaps 200) cash short-reckoning. Many examples of such tablets are preserved today. Perhaps they were issued by the local government of Lin-an Fu.

2.29 Token money known as *mu-p'ai*, "wooden tablets," *chu-p'ai*, "bamboo tablets," *chiu-p'ai*, "tablets for wine," and others circulated during the Yüan period. The wooden and bamboo tablets probably represented cash and those for wine and the like apparently represented a claim for a certain amount of the commodity. These were issued by private individuals rather than by the government. In the year 1294, an imperial decree prohibited the circulation of such tablets. It is doubtful whether the decree had real effect. The use of such token tablets was continued presumably in Ming and certainly in Ch'ing times.

2.30 People who were born in the nineteenth or the early twentieth century usually can recall experiences regarding token tablets. Specimens may be found in numismatic collections. Most of the tablets were made of bamboo or wood. In some exceptional cases copper was used. The bamboo or wooden pieces were from two to four inches long, one-third to two-thirds of an inch wide, with a hole near the top. The copper ones were considerably smaller. They bore carved or written characters indicating the amount of cash they represented, the name and address of the issuing party, and occasionally a serial number. The amount ranged from 1 to 1000 cash, sometimes in full count, but more frequently in discounted strings. For instance, 6, 8, 12, or 20 might be deducted from each thousand, and the rate of discount was always specified on the tablet. The issuing party was usually a shop of reputation, but not necessarily a money shop. In some cases, the tablet bore the words of explanation: *Yin-ch'ien-pu-fu, ch'üan-i-ch'ou-tai,* "Because of a shortage of cash, tablets are temporarily used as a substitute." Obviously these token tablets had only small areas of circulation, probably limited to a small part of the city.

2.31 Some token tablets did not represent cash but rather a claim or a right. For instance, a storyteller might distribute tablets to his audience as tickets, a water carrier to his customers as tokens for pails of water, the keeper of a public men's room to visitors as admission charge. These tablets were often sold at a lower price when they were purchased in larger quantities. The arrangement is similar to the tokens for rides on buses or trolley cars in American cities.

Round Coins from Antiquity to the End of the Ch'ing Dynasty

(1) From Antiquity to the End of the Former Han Dynasty

3.1 A semilegendary tradition dates the beginning of round copper coins in early Chou times. The *History of the Former Han Dynasty* tells us that T'ai-kung, a senior statesman who aided in the founding of the Chou kingdom, introduced the monetary system known as *chiu-fu yüan-fa* for the new dynasty. Commentators identify the *chiu-fu* as nine offices mentioned in the *Chou-li* and understand the term *yüan-fa* as a system of round coins or simply a currency system. There is little doubt that Pan Ku, the author of the *History of the Former Han Dynasty*, attributed the invention of the round coin to T'ai-kung, because, elaborating on the *chiu-fu yüan-fa,* the historian added, "coins were round with a square hole [in the middle], and their weight went by *shu.* . . . After T'ai-kung retired (from service at the court of Chou and was made the duke of Ch'i) he also set up [this financial system] for practice in [the feudatory of] Ch'i."

3.2 Modern scholars, however, refuse to accept this semilegendary account as historical. The identification of *chiu-fu* with the nine offices in the *Chou-li* is doubtful, because the nine were arbitrarily put together by the commentators from different parts of the *Chou-li*. There is no evidence that the *chiu-fu* were offices in the Chou court. A more reliable tradition of Han times says that the Ch'i statesman Kuan Chung established the *chiu-fu* or nine offices to control products of mountains and seas and that the work *Kuan-tzŭ* attributed to his authorship once contained a chapter called *chiu-fu,* possibly on coinage. It seems that the *chiu-fu* was a Ch'i institution and was not necessarily borrowed from Chou. The interpretation of *chiu-fu* as related to currency and the attribution of the invention of the round coin to T'ai-kung, however, may have reflected early coinage in general, rather than early round coins in particular, in the state of Ch'i. Certain knife coins of Ch'i can be traced back to the last decades of the fifth century B.C. and may be considered the first coins issued by a state authority instead of by private merchants.

3.3 Another doubtful account in the same history is the story about the issue of large coins bearing the words *pao-huo,* "precious currency," by King Ching of Chou in 524 B.C. The description reads: "In shape they were round with a square hole in the center, and all had a raised rim around [both inner and outer] edges." Numismatists have tried to identify this early coin which bore a two-character inscription. There are specimens bearing inscriptions which might be read *pao-huo, pao-ssŭ-huo,* and *pao-liu-huo.* The reading of the character *pao* in these inscriptions, however, is uncertain, because the character may very well be *Yen* (a state in modern Hopei), *I* (a town in modern Shantung), or an unidentified place name. These specimens can be assigned with any certainty only to the later part of the period of Warring States (481–221 B.C.).

3.4 Earliest round coins probably bore a round hole rather than a square one. There are preserved specimens of these round hole coins. The legends on them refer to their places of origin, value, or weight, and the style of the legends is very similar to the inscriptions on spade coins, especially the "round-foot" type. The round coin may have been derived from the round-foot spade money. It is unlikely that it was modeled after the ring in the handle of the knife coins.

3.5 The first round coin belonging to a united China was the *pan-liang,* which circulated first in the Ch'in state and later throughout the whole empire. Like later round coins, it had a square hole. Its weight was probably half an ounce or twelve *shu* as its legend indicates. When the short Ch'in dynasty was overthrown, Kao-tsu, the founder of the Han dynasty, found the Ch'in *pan-liang* too heavy for practical use. Moreover, he disapproved of government monopoly of coinage, which the Ch'in had imposed. Thus he relaxed the coinage laws, permitting the use of coins of lighter weight and private mints. The result was a decrease in the size and weight of coins to such a degree that they were informally referred to as *yü-chia ch'ien,* "elm-pod" money.

3.6 By the time of Empress Lü, the problem of underweight coins had become serious. Consequently in 186 B.C. she prohibited private coinage, and minted a *pan-liang* coin, which weighed 8 *shu,* two-thirds of its nominal weight. This may have been found too heavy, because three years later, in 183 B.C., she had a *wu-fên* coin minted weighing one-fifth of half an ounce (*pan-liang*) or 2.4 *shu.* Considering the *wu-fên* coin too light, Emperor Wên in 175 B.C. issued a coin weighing 4 *shu*. The 4-*shu* coin was also known as *san-fên ch'ien,* i.e., "one-third" of one-half ounce. These various coins, although different in weight, all bore the same inscription, *pan-liang.*

3.7 The 4-*shu* coin circulated for approximately fifty years, except for a short interval from 140 to 136 B.C. when a return was made to a 3-*shu* coin. By the middle of the reign of Emperor Wu (140–87 B.C.) campaigns against northern barbarians and floods of the Yellow River had almost exhausted the government treasury. New fiscal measures had to be taken and these included reforms of currency. In 119 B.C. the 4-*shu pan-liang* coins were withdrawn and melted down. A new 3-*shu* coin was issued bearing a legend indicating its actual weight. The 3-*shu* coin, as a unit of cash, was lighter than the 4-*shu pan-liang,* and thus represented an inflationary force. Another significant feature of the 3-*shu* was that it was the first Han coin the legend of which indicated its actual weight. It was time to do away with the conventional but inaccurate legend *pan-liang.*

3.8 In 118 B.C. the 3-*shu* coin was replaced by a 5-*shu* coin whose legend also indicated its actual weight. At first it was issued by both central and local authorities, but from 113 B.C. on only by the central mints under the *san-kuan,* "three offices," in the imperial park Shang-lin. The 5-*shu* coin was cast in such a way that counterfeiting became unprofitable. Consequently it proved even more stable than the 4-*shu* coin. As a matter of fact, it lasted far beyond the Han dynasty.

3.9 The Han government for over a century had experimented with coins weighing one-fifth to two-thirds of the Chin *pan-liang,* in other words, from 2.4 to 8 *shu*. It also hesitated in adopting a harsh policy against private coinage. At last 5-*shu* proved to be a convenient unit of cash and government monopoly the solution of the coinage problem. In the 123 years after 118 B.C. the total number of coins cast is said to have been more than twenty-eight billion.

(2) *From Wang Mang to the End of the Six Dynasties*

3.10 A discontinuation of the 5-*shu* coin as the sole standard of copper cash came at the beginning of the Christian era. In 7 A.D., when he was still a regent for the Han emperor, Wang Mang established three new currencies which were to circulate along with the 5-*shu* coin. These were the gold-inlaid knife coin or *chin-ts'o-tao* valued at 5000 cash or 5-*shu* pieces, the inscribed knife coin or *ch'i-tao* valued at 500 cash, and the round coin which bore the inscription *ta-ch'üan wu-shih,* "big coin value 50 (cash)."

3.11 When Wang Mang finally usurped the throne, in 9 A.D., he abolished the 5-*shu* currency and the two knife coins. He rejected the 5-*shu* coin because it was the standard coin of the Han dynasty, and the two knife coins because they could be interpreted as being related to, or symbolic of, the Han imperial surname *Liu,* the character for which contains the characters *chin-tao,* "metal knife." To replace these Wang introduced the *ch'üan* and *pu,* round coins and spade coins, claiming that he was reverting to the Chou terminology of currency. There were six varieties of *ch'üan: hsiao-ch'üan chih-i,* "petty coin value one," *yao-ch'üan i-shih,* "baby cash value ten," *yu-ch'üan êrh-shih,* "adolescent coin value twenty," *chung-ch'üan san-shih,* "medium coin value thirty," *chuang-ch'üan ssǔ-shih,* "adult coin value forty," and *ta-ch'üan wu-shih.* There were ten denominations of *pu,* the smallest worth 100 cash and the others each increasing by one hundred to the largest, which represented 1000 cash. In addition, Wang Mang defined four kinds of money made from tortoise shell, five from cowry, two from silver, and one from gold. The people, however, found the new system too confusing, and it was eventually abandoned, except for the *hsiao-ch'üan chih-i* and *ta-ch'üan wu-shih.*

3.12 After 14 A.D. the two round coins, the one petty and the other big, were demonetized. In their stead, a spade coin with the legend *huo-pu,* "currency spade," and a round coin *huo-ch'üan,* "currency coin," were issued. The *huo-ch'üan* was the unit of one cash and *huo-pu* twenty-five. The former actually weighed 5 *shu* and in reality represented a return to the Han practice.

3.13 Dissatisfied with the complicated series of currency issued by Wang Mang, the people prayed for the return of the 5-*shu* coin. A ballad at the time said, "The yellow cow has a white belly; the 5-*shu* coin will return." It returned with the Latter Han and lasted about four centuries beyond it. Round coins of very large denominations were issued in the beginning of the Six Dynasties and those of various size were in circulation in this period of disunion. But the 5-*shu* remained the basic unit and several coins issued by rulers in both North and South China bore the same legend.

3.14 An interesting point is that Wang Mang used the word *ch'üan* ("spring; currency") in all of his six round coins. As a name for coins in general and round coins in particular, *ch'üan* is synonymous with *ch'ien,* the preferred expression from Han times down. But since *ch'üan* is used in the *Chou-li,* which was supposed to contain ancient institutions of the

Chou dynasty, it is natural that the antiquarian Wang Mang should have chosen the term.

3.15 In this connection, we may point out an earlier meaning of *ch'ien*, namely, an agricultural implement. In the *Book of Odes* there are lines which have been translated as follows:

> "Order our multitude:
> 'Prepare your spades and hoes';
> Everywhere we shall see the sickles mow."

The poem can be dated at the beginning of the first millennium B.C. The Chinese words translated as "spades" and "hoes" are *ch'ien* and *p'u*. The ancient spade money *pu* is undoubtedly related to the *p'u* in the text. *Ch'ien*, later used to mean "coin," obviously indicated the metal piece of a hoe, as evidenced also in other ancient texts.

(3) From the T'ang Dynasty to the End of the Ch'ing Dynasty

3.16 In the early part of the seventh century a new era of round coins was ushered in with the unification of China by the T'ang dynasty. In 621, a coin was issued bearing a legend of four characters at the four sides of the square hole instead of to the left and right of the hole as in the case of *pan-liang* and 5-*shu*. This was by no means the first coin with a four-character legend because sporadic examples existed already during the Six Dynasties. The legend is important because it furnished subsequent coins with two elements, *yüan-pao*, "principal treasure," and *t'ung-pao*, "circulating treasure," resulting from two different ways of reading the whole legend, as *K'ai-t'ung yüan-pao* or *K'ai-yüan t'ung-pao*.

3.17 *K'ai-t'ung yüan-pao* resulted from *huan-tu*, reading clockwise from the top, and it seems to have been the official reading. It probably meant something like "Principal treasure which opens (a new era) and circulates." The popular reading was *K'ai-yüan t'ung-pao*, "Circulating treasure which opens a new era." This result was obtained from *tui-tu*, reading from top to bottom and right to left. From the eighth century on, the two compounds, *yüan-pao* and *t'ung-pao*, were used after reign titles of emperors to form a four-character legend. The practice was so common that many people have mistaken the *K'ai-yüan t'ung-pao* as containing the reign title *K'ai-yüan* which is, of course, an anachronism.

3.18 The compound *yüan-pao* was later borrowed in the name *yüan-pao ch'ao*, a paper currency of the Yüan period. Since paper money often used silver as its reserve, the term *yüan-pao* from Yüan times on acquired a new meaning, referring to an ingot of shoe-shaped silver. Possibly to avoid confusion, *t'ung-pao* became the standard element to follow a reign title in the legend on coins of Ming and Ch'ing dynasties.

3.19 In addition to its composition, the *K'ai-yüan t'ung-pao* coin was significant for its weight, one *ch'ien,* "mace," or one tenth of a *liang.* According to earlier reckoning, one *liang* contained 24 *shu.* Thus one *ch'ien* should be only 2.4 *shu.* Actually the *K'ai-yüan t'ung-pao* was 44 per cent heavier than the Han 5-*shu,* because a T'ang ounce was three times as heavy as the Han ounce. A heavier ounce and a new unit, the mace, were two major changes in weights under the T'ang dynasty. Both were to last throughout the imperial era of Chinese history. From this time on, the word *ch'ien* acquired the double meaning of a coin and a mace.

3.20 The *K'ai-t'ung yüan-pao* or *K'ai-yüan t'ung-pao* had three imitations which resembled it closely. The last two of the Five Dynasties, Han and Chou, issued coins bearing respectively the legends *Han-t'ung yüan-pao* and *Chou-t'ung yüan-pao.* The founder of the Sung dynasty introduced the *Sung-t'ung yüan-pao.* Each of the three coins contains the name of the ruling dynasty and the characters *t'ung, yüan,* and *pao,* and permits another reading, *Han-yüan t'ung-pao, Chou-yüan t'ung-pao* or *Sung-yüan t'ung-pao.*

3.21 Unlike the *K'ai-yüan t'ung-pao* which was cast throughout the T'ang dynasty and circulated along with coins bearing reign titles, the *Sung-yüan t'ung-pao* was replaced after the second emperor of the dynasty by coins bearing the reign title plus the element *t'ung-pao* or *yüan-pao.* New legends were introduced not only when new emperors came to the throne but also when the ruling emperor changed his reign title to a new one. For the eighteen emperors of the Northern and Southern Sung dynasties, there were as many as fifty-one reign titles registered on coins.

3.22 The *K'ai-yüan t'ung-pao* was significant also because it opened a new era of calligraphic style on coin legends. The characters on Sui and earlier coins were generally in the *chuan-shu* or seal style. The *K'ai-yüan t'ung-pao* was in the *li-shu* or scribe style, which was less archaic than the seal style and much closer to the modern *k'ai-shu* or regular style. Sung coins bearing the reign title frequently had the same legend appearing in a series of styles, including seal, scribe, regular, and even running (*hsing-shu*) and cursive styles (*ts'ao-shu*). This series is known among numismatic collectors as *tui-ch'ien,* "matched coins." Regular style was the rule for characters on Ming and Ch'ing coins.

3.23 Certain coins were also issued by alien dynasties in China. The legends were generally in Chinese. Occasionally the coins bore non-Chinese writings like the Ch'i-tan script of Liao and the 'Phags-pa script of Yüan.

These non-Chinese legends appear either alone or in conjunction with Chinese ones. A rare Yüan specimen is known as *ssŭ-t'i ch'ien,* "coin with legends in four scripts." On one side it bears four Chinese characters, *Chih-yüan t'ung-pao,* and on the other side the same words in three other languages. The characters *Chih-yüan* are in 'Phags-pa, the character *t'ung* is in Persian, and *pao* is in Tangut script.

3.24 In the early years of the Manchu dynasty, the rulers T'ai-tsu and T'ai-tsung made coins which bore in Manchu script their respective reign titles *T'ien-ming* and *T'ien-ts'ung.* From emperor Shun-chih to the end of the dynasty, coins bore Chinese characters indicating the reign on one side and on the other Manchu letters denoting the mint. Coins made in Peking bore in Manchu script the words *Pao-ch'üan* and *Pao-yüan,* names of the two government mints in the capital. Those minted in the provinces bore the word *pao* in Manchu script and another word indicating the place.

3.25 Neighbors of China also borrowed the cultural trait of round coins with a square hole. The earliest example in Japan was a coin of 708 bearing the characters *Ho-t'ung k'ai-pao* (sometimes interpreted as *Ho-t'ung k'ai-chên*). In Annam the *T'ai-p'ing hsing-pao* of 970 and *T'ien-fu chên-pao* of 980 were the first two coins of this type, and in Korea the *Hai-tung t'ung-pao* of 1102 was among the earliest. Since these countries had borrowed the Chinese writing, their coins bore legends in Chinese characters. These coins rarely found their way into China. A major exception was the Japanese *K'uan-yung t'ung-pao,* which were smuggled into eighteenth and nineteenth century China and circulated in mixed strings in considerable quantities.

3.26 The long tradition of round coins with square holes was broken in 1898 when copper coins of a new model called *t'ung-yüan* were first minted in the province of Kwangtung. In the next year an imperial decree encouraged other provinces along the coast or the Yangtse River to follow the Kwangtung example in order to ease the shortage of the old copper cash. These new coins were coined by machine and bore no holes. Most of them were made to represent 10 old copper cash. Other denominations ranged from 1 to 100 cash.

3.27 In the first few years of its existence the new copper coin was welcomed by the people as a convenient substitute for the old copper cash. Almost immediately, however, this favorable response was seized as an opportunity for the government to use the mint as a solution of fiscal problems. Central and local authorities rivaled each other in the manufacture of the new copper coin. By the early years of the Republic there was already an over-supply of *t'ung-yüan*. According to government statistics, the new copper coins in circulation were valued at approximately 292,000,000 silver dollars in 1912 and approximately 466,000,000 silver dollars in 1917. The total number of copper coins was about 29,000,000,000 in 1912 and about 41,000,000,000 in 1917. Ninety per cent of the coins were in the denomination of 10 old copper cash.

3.28 As a result of oversupply there was a continuous decline in the value of the new copper coin vis-à-vis the silver dollar. In the first decade of the new copper coin, its rate of exchange to the silver dollar was approximately 100 to 1. In the second decade to 1919 the rate changed gradually to 120–130 to 1, and in the 1920's to as high as 150–300 to 1. By this time, the old copper cash with square holes had long been driven out of circulation on account of its high intrinsic value.

(4) Gold, Silver, Iron, and Lead Coins

3.29 In Chinese history, round coins were made not only from copper but also from other materials. Gold and silver coins, or *chin-yin ch'ien*, were occasionally cast in the model of the copper cash. These were generally used as a gift or toy but not as a medium of exchange. An exception was the silver coins minted for Tibet after its conquest in 1792. They were round coins bearing a square hole in the middle. On one side were the four Chinese characters *Ch'ien-lung pao-tsang*, "Treasure for Tibet in the Ch'ien-lung era," and additional characters indicating the years. On the other side were the same words in Tibetan script. There were three denominations weighing 1.5, 1, and 0.5 mace. Similar *pao-tsang* coins were cast in the reigns of Chia-ch'ing, Tao-kuang, and Hsien-fêng.

3.30 Coins of debased metals like lead and iron were used as money in different times. Their circulation rendered it very difficult to maintain the copper cash as the uniform medium of exchange for small transactions and created many other problems. Iron coins, or *t'ieh-ch'ien*, first appeared in the Szechwan area in the early years of the Christian era when Kung-sun Shu, the local ruler, cast iron 5-*shu* pieces and put them into circulation. These were replaced by the standard copper 5-*shu* coins under the Latter Han.

3.31 In the period of the Three Kingdoms, rulers of Shu and Wu unsuccessfully attempted the issue of iron coins in their respective kingdoms in the upper and lower valleys of the Yangtse River. In 523, under the Liang dynasty, copper coins were abandoned and iron 5-*shu* coins were cast. These attempts to circulate iron cash in south China, however, did not have any lasting effect.

3.32 A remarkable change in the currency system took place in the period of the Five Dynasties. In this period of disunion, lead and iron coins were introduced in many parts of south China. Lead coins or *ch'ien-ch'ien* first appeared in 916 in the kingdom which existed in modern Fukien. About the same time or perhaps shortly afterwards, iron coins were put into circulation in the same area. Rulers of the neighboring kingdoms in Hunan and Kwangtung quickly followed the practice. They circulated lead and iron coins in the cities and copper cash in the countryside. History says that the kingdom in Hunan profited greatly from this policy. Traders who came to the cities found the currency not worth carrying away and resorted to the purchase of commodities for exportation. The effect reminds one of the competitive depreciation of currency by modern countries in order to promote export trade. The kingdoms in modern Szechwan and Kiangsu, being wealthier than the other southern provinces, held on to copper cash for a few decades longer but eventually yielded to iron in 955 and 960 respectively.

3.33 When China was again unified by the Sung dynasty, measures were taken after 977 to call in the iron cash in the lower Yangtse valley and to circulate copper cash in its stead. A similar policy was carried out successfully for the other parts of south China but failed in the Szechwan area. This replacement was effected by retaining the newly cast copper coins in south China rather than shipping some of them to north China, as was previously done. Instead the government collected large amounts of silver from the south and circulated it throughout the empire. The failure in Szechwan was partly due to a shortage of copper ores in the area and partly due to a lack of zeal on the part of the government. It was discovered that a zone of iron cash on the border would help prevent export of copper.

3.34 From about 1040 large copper coins and large and small iron coins were circulated in the Shensi and Shansi area to finance war against the Hsi-Hsia. As far as currency was concerned, the Northern Sung empire was divided into three regions: the region of iron coins in Szechwan, the region of iron and copper coins in Shansi and Shensi, and the region of copper coins in the remaining areas of China. Of the twenty-six mints which operated around 1080 under the Northern Sung, nine were devoted to producing a yearly output of 889,234,000 iron coins. Thus iron cash played a prominent role in the currency of Sung China.

3.35 The Southern Sung dynasty continued to designate Szechwan as the region of iron cash and marked a protective zone in the Huai valley by circulating both iron and copper coins in that region. Iron coins, however, ceased to be important after this period. Paper currency and silver eventually solved the problem of the shortage of copper. It was hardly necessary to resort to iron coins as a means of government finance, and it was only during a period of dire financial straits that the Ch'ing dynasty minted some in 1859.

IV

Some General Problems concerning Round Coins

(1) Government Coinage and Private Coinage

4.1 During the long period of imperial China private coinage or *ssŭ-chu* was permitted only for very short periods and in very few cases. Private coinage, known as *fang-chu*, was permitted in the early decades of the Han dynasty. History reports that in the reign of Emperor Wên (179–157 B.C.) coins of the Prince of Wu and Têng T'ung, a favorite servant of the Emperor, circulated all over the empire. The Confucian scholar Chia I objected strongly to free coinage. In a proposal, he listed three disadvantages of it and seven advantages of state coinage, but the Emperor refused to listen. In 112 B.C., Emperor Wu made coinage a state monopoly. This example of *kuan-chu* or government coinage was followed by rulers of the Han and subsequent dynasties. Government mints were established in the capital or provinces or both. These were known as *ch'ien-chien*, "coinage supervisories," in T'ang and Sung times and *ch'ien-chü*, "coinage bureaus," in the Ming and Ch'ing dynasties.

4.2 Exceptions to exclusive government coinage were few. One was in 491 when the coin *T'ai-ho wu-shu* was issued by the Northern Wei dynasty. Government mints were made available to private individuals who wished to use their own copper to cast money in the model of the new coin. A similar permission was granted by the government from 529 to 530. Two other cases also occurred in the period of the Northern and Southern Dynasties: the Sung dynasty permitted private coinage in 465 and the Eastern Wei in 548. A later example was the Latter Chin, one of the Five Dynasties, which allowed free coinage from 938 to 939. These periods of relaxation of exclusive coinage rights were invariably very short.

4.3 From Han to Tang times, scholars occasionally argued for free coinage but they were always in favor of a standard coin to avoid a chaotic state in currency. An interesting proposal was made in 548 under the Eastern Wei, successor of the Northern Wei dynasty. According to the proposal, 5-*shu* should be established the legal weight of a copper cash and only coins which met this standard be permitted to circulate. Two scales should be placed at the gate of every market place and the private scales be corrected in accordance with these official scales. Private coinage was not to be prohibited but only coins weighing 5-*shu* were to be allowed to enter the market. Debased coins containing much lead and tin should not be permitted even if they weighed 5-*shu*. Debased and light coins when discovered should be confiscated and given to reporters as awards. This proposal, however, seems to have been shelved after a court discussion. The policy of checking debased coins during their circulation was adopted by both Sui and T'ang dynasties, when sample coins called *ch'ien-yang* were posted in market places and given to officers of customs barriers. Coins different from the sample coins were not allowed to enter or pass. Of course, it is difficult to ascertain to what degree the regulation was enforced.

4.4 The right to cast a limited amount of cash was occasionally granted to a few privileged persons. The founder of the Sui dynasty granted three imperial princes the right to establish *lu*, or "hearths," to cast coins in their principalities. One prince was granted five hearths in 590, and his number was raised to ten when five hearths were allowed to each of two other princes in 598. The founder of the T'ang dynasty permitted two of his sons to establish three hearths each and a favorite minister one hearth for coinage. The T'ang emperor Hsuan-tsung allowed his barbarian general An Lu-shan to operate five hearths in his commandery. Presumably each of the hearths produced a definite number of coins just like those of the government mints. History reports that in the middle of the T'ang dynasty in 752 the government mints operated 99 hearths, of which each cast 3,300,000 cash in a year.

4.5 Counterfeiting of coins is referred to in history as *tao-chu*, "theft cast," and *ssŭ-chu*, "secret cast." The first term appears frequently in texts of Han times and the second in texts of later days. The term *ssŭ-chu* is also used to mean "private coinage" and not necessarily as a term of abuse. Debased coins were known as *o-ch'ien*, "bad money," in contrast with *hao-ch'ien*, "good money." With reference to their weight, coins were also known as *ch'ing-ch'ien*, "light money," and *chung-ch'ien*, "heavy money." Counterfeited pieces were as a rule debased and light.

4.6 Counterfeiting of coins was a crime. The government from the Han dynasty on generally made it subject to capital punishment. Occasionally, even members of the offender's family and his neighbors were also held responsible. Prizes were offered to those who reported offenses. The regulations, however, were not always carried out to the letter. Next to illegal casting was the offense of *chien-tso* or *chien-ts'o*, "cutting or chiseling" of metal from good coins. This was normally punishable by beatings. To prevent cutting and chiseling, legal coins from 115 B.C. as a rule had had raised rims called *chou-kuo*, "encircling walls."

4.7 Profit by counterfeiting was derived from mixture with such debased ingredients as lead, tin, iron, and even sand. Coins containing an excessive proportion of lead and tin were known as *ch'ien-hsi ch'ien*. They were particularly numerous in T'ang and Sung times in spite of government prohibition. Coins mixed with sand were known as *sha-wei ch'ien*, "sand-tailed money," in the Sung period and *sha-pan*, "sand plates," in Ch'ing times. There were spurious iron coins as well as copper ones. Counterfeiting often proved profitable when the government put into circulation coins of very large denominations.

4.8 Counterfeiting was occasionally carried out on a large scale and in a semiopen manner. Toward the end of the Northern Sung dynasty, it was estimated that there were over 100,000 counterfeiters in the country. In the Shensi area, a policy was adopted by the government to enlist expert counterfeiters and members of their families, to cast coins in places called *chu-ch'ien yüan*, "coinage courts," which actually resembled concentration camps. It is not known how successful this policy of conversion proved to be. Imperial princes of the Ming dynasty and Bannermen of the Manchu dynasty were sometimes connected with the manufacture of spurious coins because these privileged people were beyond the reach of ordinary police. In the latter part of the Ch'ing period, debased coins were produced even in government mints. These were known by the ironical name of *chü-ssŭ*, literally, "bureau counterfeit," i.e., illegal coins made by a *ch'ien-chü* or coinage bureau.

4.9 Another illegal practice, *ssŭ-hsiao* or "secret melting," is closely connected with *ssŭ-chu*, "secret cast," because the former often provided material for the latter. However, secret melting was also practiced alone when the ingredients contained in a coin became more valuable than its face value. In T'ang and Sung times, coins were secretly destroyed to make brass articles which were in great demand. In order to check the practice, the government repeatedly prohibited the use of brass utensils beyond a certain limit. These prohibitions, however, did not prove as powerful as the natural economic forces of demand and supply.

(2) *Single and Multiple Denominations*

4.10 The term *tzŭ-mu hsiang-ch'üan,* literally "mutual balance between mother and child," referred to concurrent circulation of coins of different denominations, which were usually of different size and weight. The *ta-ch'ien,* "large coins," and *chung-ch'ien,* "heavy coins," were compared to the mother; and *hsiao-ch'ien,* "small coins," and *ch'ing-ch'ien,* "light coins," to the son. The concept of the mutual balance between the two is first found in the *Kuo-yü* in a passage dealing with the minting of large coins by King Ching of Chou in 524 B.C. According to *Shih-chi* 119.1a-b, currency of large denominations was issued about one century earlier by King Chuang of Ch'u (613–591 B.C.). According to a less creditable work, *I Chou shu* 11, the device of using large and small coins concurrently was already discovered by King Wên at the beginning of Chou times. Modern scholars, however consider these records legendary or semilegendary, perhaps made up in the time of Warring States when coins of different denominations, size, and weight were in circulation.

4.11 In the history of coinage in China, there were two different trends: one preferred a single standard coin and the other favored concurrent use of coins of different denominations. The 5-*shu* coin of the Han dynasty was a typical example of the former, whereas the complicated series of currency issued by Wang Mang constituted an extreme case of the latter. Actually, Wang Mang, in the introduction of his currency reforms, claimed to be returning to the Chou principle of "mutual balance between mother and child." Founders of subsequent dynasties as a rule established as standard only a single denomination of round coin. Their successors, however, often were induced by the profit of larger and heavier coins of disproportionately high value. They found in the ancient device of *tzŭ-mu hsiang-ch'üan* a convenient excuse for their inflationary measures.

4.12 In this connection, it may be pointed out that, although *ch'ing-ch'ien* and *chung-ch'ien* generally meant light and heavy coins, the expressions *ch'ien-ch'ing* and *ch'ien-chung* were rather ambiguous. *Ch'ing* may have meant light or having a small purchasing power; and *chung* heavy or of high value. A term *ch'üan ch'ing-chung* was used in old texts to refer to the maintenance of a balance between money and commodities by means of government control. The principle was attributed to the statesman Kuan Chung of Ch'i. The use of the word *ch'üan* "to balance; to weigh" in the phrases of *tzŭ-mu hsiang-ch'üan* and *ch'üan ch'ing-chung* indicates an understanding of the necessity of a proper balance between the demand and supply of different kinds of money, or money and commodities.

4.13 After the introduction of paper currency, the term *tzŭ-mu hsiang-ch'üan* acquired three more meanings. One referred to paper money as *tzŭ* or child, and its reserve, in silver or copper coins, as *mu* or mother. Under the Yüan dynasty, reserves of paper currency were known as *ch'ao-mu* as well as *ch'ao-pên*. Another use of *tzŭ-mu hsiang-ch'üan* was apparently the reverse of the first meaning. It took coins to be *tzŭ* and paper money to be *mu*. This is understandable because a paper note ordinarily was in a denomination larger than a single coin. The third meaning denoted paper money of large and small denominations respectively as *mu* and *tzŭ*. All three meanings are attested in texts of Yüan times. The last one was most in accordance with the traditional use of the term and consequently was considered by certain contemporaries as the only orthodox usage.

4.14 Coins of large denominations as a rule were larger and heavier than those of small denominations. The difference in size and weight, however, was not necessarily proportional to the difference in value. A recognizable mark was sufficient to distinguish a coin of higher value. For instance, the *ch'ih-ts'ê* or "red rim" coin was issued by Emperor Wu of the Han dynasty in 115 B.C. It was of the same size as the ordinary 5-*shu* coin and bore the same legend. Its red rim however, raised its value to five times that of the ordinary 5-*shu*. More often, a difference was indicated in the legend. Certain spade coins of the Warring States bore a small character, *liang* or *êrh*, "two," to indicate that they represented twice the value of an ordinary spade coin of the same kind. Many coins issued by Wang Mang bore inscriptions indicating their value. This is true also with coins of large denominations in later times. These coins were known as *chê-êrh*, "equal to two," *chê-san*, "equal to three," *tang-wu*, "representing five," *tang-shih*, "representing ten," etc. In contrast, the standard coin valued at one cash was called *hsiao-p'ing-ch'ien*. In Sung times, this term referred to standard coins like the *Sung-t'ung yüan-pao*. Numismatists of later times also use the term to indicate standard one-cash coins of other dynasties. One expression often found on coins of large denominations is *chung-pao*, literally "heavy treasure." The first coin bearing this legend was the *Ch'ien-yüan chung-pao* of 758. It was valued at ten times the standard *K'ai-t'ung yüan-pao* of the T'ang dynasty.

(3) *Full and Short Strings*

4.15 Round coins in large sums were reckoned by strings. In Chinese, the terms for a string were *min, kuan, tiao,* and *ch'uan*. The first two were frequently used during the Sung and earlier times, and the other two prevailed in the Ming and Ch'ing periods. In theory a string should contain one thousand cash, but in actual transactions a smaller number was often accepted.

4.16 Toward the end of the Manchu dynasty and in the early years of the Chinese Republic, there was a proverb describing the natives of Peking as *shuo-ta-hua, shih-hsiao-ch'ien,* literally, "speak big words, but use small cash." The expression *hsiao-ch'ien* here referred to what may be termed "short strings," and not to coins of small size, because in Peking ten modern round copper coins (called *t'ung-yüan,* or colloquially, *t'ung-tzŭ-êrh*) were reckoned as a *tiao* or a string of one thousand. Since ten modern copper coins represented only one hundred copper cash (*chih-ch'ien*), the *tiao* of one thousand corresponded to only one hundred cash. Hence the proverb. **1168841**

4.17 Practice of similar nature was not limited to Peking, and its history went back to at least the second century of the Christian era. The people in Peking perhaps deserved this satirical remark, because they carried the practice to an extreme. In the early Republican years, as I recall it, in Paoting which was only about one hundred miles to the southwest of Peking, 48 to 50 modern copper coins were reckoned as a *tiao.* There the string was shortened to about one-half, whereas in Peking it was reduced to one-tenth of the full string.

4.18 A survey made in 1889 revealed that 480–500 cash formed the *tiao* in several provinces in north China, including Chihli (Hopei), Shantung, Shansi, and Shensi. In central and south China, short strings were called *chiu-pa ch'ien,* "980 cash string," *chiu-liu ch'ien,* "960 cash string," and so forth. Thus a cash was still a cash in these provinces, but it represented two coins in the string in northern provinces. This difference in reckoning apparently affected only the nominal prices of commodities but not their real exchange value. For instance, a tael of silver would exchange for about twice the amount of cash in north China in order to compensate for the difference in reckoning.

4.19 Because of this difference, the degree of fullness of the string was specified for transactions in terms of cash and on credit instruments. In Manchuria, a particularly small string was used in the nineteenth century, which contained about 160 cash. It was known as *hsiao-shu ch'ien,* "small reckoning cash," and it was counted by the *ch'uan* rather than the *tiao.* Financial authorities in Peking had to keep separate accounts for cash paid and received in Manchuria and that in China proper to avoid confusion. The short strings in north China and Manchuria probably indicated a relative scarcity of cash in these areas.

4.20 The fact that short strings existed in the second century is not recorded in history but revealed from two preserved contracts on the purchase of land. These were lead pieces of about one and a half Chinese feet in length and one and a half inch in width. Characters were inscribed on either one side or on both sides to represent the contract. From one contract of 184 and another of 188, we find the inscriptions concluding with the same phrase, *ch'ien-ch'ien-wu-wu-shih,* meaning "The cash is short of 50 per thousand." Evidently a 950 cash string was in use.

4.21 The fourth century work *Pao-p'u tzŭ* contains the line *chieh-jên ch'ang-ch'ien, huan-jên tuan-pai,* "to borrow in long strings and to pay back in short ones." This, of course, was considered immoral. The terms *ch'ang-ch'ien,* "long strings," and *tuan-pai,* "short strings" (literally, "short hundreds"), are here contrasted with each other. The two characters for *ch'ang-ch'ien,* however, have other readings and meanings. In *Shih-chi* 129, they seem to read *chang-ch'ien* and have the meaning "to increase the nominal exchange value of cash." The phrase *chang-ch'ien shan-chia* is found in the first-century work *I-lin,* and may be translated as "to have high exchange value of cash (when buying) and to receive good prices (when selling)"; in other words, ideal conditions for a businessman. It is, however, not impossible that the phrase may read *ch'ang-ch'ien shan-chia* to mean "selling at good prices and receiving full strings." In modern spoken Chinese the rise of prices of commodities is referred to as *chang-ch'ien.* This meaning, however, does not apply in ancient texts.

4.22 Under the Liang dynasty in the fifth century, in the eastern part of south China 80 coins and in the western part 70 coins were accepted as "100." The reckonings were known respectively as *tung-ch'ien,* "eastern cash," and *hsi-ch'ien,* "western cash." In the capital, Nanking, 90 coins were reckoned as "100," and this was called *ch'ang-ch'ien,* "long (string of) cash." In 546, the Emperor ordered the use of *tsu-pai* or "full 100" strings. This rule, however, was not enforced, and toward the end of the dynasty, as few as 35 coins were accepted as "100."

4.23 From the middle of the T'ang period, the government found it necessary to regulate the various ways of reckoning short strings. In 821 a decree defined a *kuan* or string as 920 cash. The 80 cash deduction was called *ch'u-pai* or *ch'u-tien.* Toward the end of the dynasty, in 906, the official string contained 850 cash. In the period of the Five Dynasties, the string was shortened to 800 cash in 927, and to 770 in 948. The Sung dynasty accepted

77 cash as "100" and called it *shêng-pai* or simply *shêng*. In contrast, the full "100" was called *tsu-pai* or simply *tsu*. The terms *shêng* and *tsu* were used regularly in accounts of the period. For instance, *san-pai-wên-tsu* indicates full strings of 300 cash but *san-pai-wên-shêng* means "300 cash in short strings," i.e., actually 231 coins. The Chin dynasty reckoned 88 cash as "100." Short strings were used in later dynasties, although the government did not bother to define the sum.

(4) The Copper Problem

4.24 As indicated by the name *t'ung-ch'ien,* "copper coin," the standard cash had copper as its main component. Other common ingredients were tin, lead, and zinc. The proportion of the metals varied in different periods. Generally speaking, there was a tendency in later dynasties to reduce the proportion of copper. Another tendency in Ming and Ch'ing times was to use no tin but a large proportion of zinc in the alloy. In other words, more brass coins than bronze coins were minted, although the reverse was true in earlier periods.

4.25 Chemical analysis of coins of Western Han and Wang Mang times reveals that copper formed 75–90 per cent of the alloy. Tin and zinc together formed 6–9 per cent. The amount of lead was indefinite, ranging from 0.5 to 12.5 per cent. Metallic content of the T'ang standard coin is reported for 752. The alloy contained approximately 83 per cent copper, 15 per cent lead, and 2 per cent tin. In 1019 under the Sung dynasty, the alloy of the standard coin consisted of approximately 64 per cent copper, 27 per cent lead, and 9 per cent tin. In the Ming period, bronze coins contained approximately 91 per cent copper and 9 per cent tin; and brass coins 90 per cent copper and 10 per cent zinc. The alloy of bronze coins of the Ch'ing dynasty consisted of approximately 50 per cent copper, 41.5 per cent zinc, 6.5 per cent lead and 2 per cent tin. The Ch'ing brass coins were made of half copper and half zinc. In Ch'ing and earlier times, bronze coins were referred to by their color as *ch'ing-ch'ien,* "green coins," and brass ones as *huang-ch'ien,* "yellow coins." As a rule, "green coins" were preferred to "yellow coins."

4.26 Since coinage of cash was a government monopoly for the most part of imperial China, the government took great care in assuring its copper supply. Mining of copper was under strict control. A major portion of copper production went to the government by way of percentage taxation and compulsory purchase. Manufacture of copper articles was subject to restriction. Melting of coins to obtain copper for utensils was prohibited. Export of coins was against the law, and sometimes hoarding of excessive amounts of cash was also forbidden by law. When there was a shortage, the people were encouraged to turn in their copper utensils to the government to be melted for coinage. Even Buddhist statues made of copper were occasionally destroyed on the excuse that the benevolent Buddha probably would not mind sacrificing his statues to save the people.

4.27   Copper shortage was particularly serious in the two Sung periods. Contemporaries referred to the shortage as *ch'ien-huang,* "coin famine." Actually the Sung dynasty minted more coins than any of the other dynasties in Chinese history. Development of international trade in this period, however, had made Sung coins a generally acceptable medium of exchange all over the Far East. Legal and smuggled export of Sung cash must have been a considerable drain. In the words of an eleventh-century official, "Cash was originally the treasure of China, but its use is now shared with the various barbarians." Excavations of large amounts of Sung coins in Japan and the South Sea countries in modern times offer ample proof of this fact. The copper shortage in Sung times of course was closely related to the use of iron coins and paper currency.

4.28   Generally speaking, most copper mines were in South China. The three famous centers of copper mining in Northern Sung times were Shao-chou in modern Kwangtung, T'an-chou in modern Hunan, and Hsin-chou in modern Kiangsi. In the middle of the eleventh century the output from Shao-chou was so large that for a short period the government even relaxed the prohibition on export of copper cash. Outside of mining, the Sung dynasty also attempted to reclaim copper from copper compounds, which were found in wells and other places. Copper so obtained was called *tan-t'ung, tan* referring to *tan-shui* ($CuSO_4 + 5H_2O$), which was necessary for the reclamation process. The Sung dynasty probably also imported copper from Korea and Japan, but apparently not in very substantial quantities.

4.29   Japanese copper, known as *yang-t'ung,* "foreign copper," was essential in Ming and Ch'ing times. Chinese merchants were encouraged and even dispatched to Japan to trade for copper. China's dependence on "foreign copper" was especially acute during the first quarter of the eighteenth century, when Ch'ing mints subsisted solely on imports from Japan. The copper mines from Yunnan, however, already assumed importance beginning with the seventeenth century. From 1738, *Tien-t'ung* (or Yunnan copper) began to meet the need of the two central mints, *Hu-pu pao-ch'üan-chü* and *Kung-pu pao-yüan-chü* in Peking.

4.30 China, however, did not become entirely independent of Japanese copper. From 1738 to 1824, the provincial mints operated on a full scale. Among the fourteen provinces where coins were minted, Szechwan was self-sufficient; Yunnan supplied itself and Kwangtung, Kwangsi, Kweichou, and Fukien. Hunan supplemented its own produce with Yunnan copper. Chihli and Shansi purchased Japanese copper from merchants. Kiangsu, Chekiang, Kiangsi, Hupeh, and Shensi received their copper partly from Yunnan and partly from Japan. Zinc, lead, and tin were produced in Kweichow and were available in the market in Hankow. After 1825 many provinces indicated the desire to reduce or cease coinage of copper because of the low exchange ratio of copper cash to silver. The cessation and reduction, which occurred also at other times, were known as *t'ing-lu chien-mao*, "to stop the hearth and to reduce the quota."

V

Gold and Silver

(*1*) *From Antiquity to the Sixth Century*

5.1 Gold and silver circulated as money throughout the long imperial era of Chinese history. Gold has been called *chin* or *huang-chin*, "yellow metal," and silver *yin* or *pai-chin*, "white metal." It is known that gold was also used in ancient China prior to its unification into the Ch'in empire in 221 B.C. Information concerning the use of silver as money in the pre-Ch'in period, however, is not available.

5.2 There are many references to the use of *chin* in pre-Ch'in China as metallic money by weight. Interpretation of these references, however, is uncertain because the word *chin* in ancient texts has three meanings, namely, gold, copper, and metal in general. The first two meanings are particularly difficult to distinguish. Only rarely does the context furnish a clue. The difficulty is further increased by the probability that the same unit of weight may have been applied to different metals. This apparently was the case with gold and copper in ancient China.

5.3 A very ancient unit of weight is *lieh* or *yüan*. The two characters have been identified as variant names for the same unit. *Lieh* appears in bronze inscriptions as early as the beginning of Chou (ca. 1027 B.C.). In one case, the King presented a prince with *chin-pai-lieh*, "one hundred *lieh* of gold (or copper)." Another case mentions a fine of *ku-san-pai-lieh*, "three hundred *lieh* according to old reckoning." This indicates that at the beginning of Chou there were already old and new ways of reckoning a *lieh*, probably based on traditions of the Shang and Chou dynasties respectively.

5.4 Important references to *yüan* (identified with *lieh*) are found in the chapter *Lü-hsing* of the *Book of History*. This chapter, attributable to the ninth century B.C., specifies the number of *yüan* in which a criminal could present metal (probably copper) to redeem his punishment. Capital punishment could be bought off with 1000 *yüan*, and lesser punishments by smaller sums. According to one tradition, a *yüan* contained 11¹³⁄₂₅ *shu,* which was supposed to represent the weight of one hundred grains of a certain kind of millet. Twenty-four *shu* made a *liang* or ounce, and sixteen *liang* made a *chin* or catty. Thus 100 *yüan* (or *lieh*) were the equivalent of three catties. Another tradition, however, equates a *yüan* or *lieh* with six *liang,* and a third tradition equates it with six and two-thirds *liang.* Of these three traditions, modern scholars prefer the first, which gives it a rather light weight. It is nevertheless possible that the three traditions may have represented regional differences or have been used at different periods. Similar discrepancies were common in later times.

5.5 The word *yüan* is actually found on the stampmark of certain ancient gold plates, which undoubtedly served as money in the southern state of Ch'u in the period of the Warring States. The stampmarks are in small squares bearing characters reading *Ying-yüan,* "Yüan of Ying," *Ch'ên-yüan,* "Yüan of Ch'ên," and *Shou-ch'un.* Ying, Ch'ên, and Shou-ch'un were three places which served as the capital of Ch'u, the first in the fourth century B.C. and earlier times and the second and the third in the third century B.C. These pieces have been unearthed occasionally in modern Anhwei since about the eleventh century. There are pieces bearing two, six, fourteen, and sixteen such square stamps. Copper and lead pieces of similar type are reported to have been discovered in the same province. Their authenticity, however, is not yet established; otherwise, we may assume the existence of a multimetallic currency in the ancient state of Ch'u.

5.6 A large unit of weight in ancient China was *i.* It was used primarily for gold in the period of Warring States. Two traditions identify the unit differently as 20 and 24 ounces. They may have indicated a regional divergence. In Han times, instead of *i,* the *chin* or catty was the unit of gold. A catty of gold was generally valued at 10,000 cash. From the Six Dynasties and the T'ang dynasty on, both gold and silver tended to be mentioned by ounce rather than by catty. This may have been the result of the high value assigned to the two precious metals in later times. The word *chin,* "metal" (not to be confused with *chin,* "catty"), appears occasionally in texts of Han or earlier date to mean a catty. In later times, however, it frequently indicates a *liang* or ounce.

5.7 Such changes in the meaning of units were by no means uncommon. For instance, the unit *i* in texts of T'ang or later date seems to indicate neither 20 nor 24 ounces, but merely one ounce. Another word *hsing* often appears in T'ang and Sung literature meaning one ounce of gold or silver. This word *hsing,* literally "star," undoubtedly comes from the stars on a stick scale. In the Ch'ing period, however, *hsing* was used to indicate a *ch'ien*, "mace," i.e., one tenth of an ounce. It may be noted that the units *chin*, "catty," *liang*, "ounce," *ch'ien*, "mace" tended to be used in their scientific meanings, whereas units like *chin*, "metal," and *hsing*, "star," tended to be used more for their literary flavor than for accuracy. This made it possible to use units of the second group in different meanings, but in each case to indicate the normal unit currently in use.

5.8 China's first recorded issue of silver currency was in the reign of Han Wu-ti. According to *Han shu* 24B the emperor in 119 B.C. put into circulation three pieces of *pai-chin*, "white metal," which was actually an alloy of silver and tin. The first piece was round in shape, weighed eight ounces, had a dragon design, and was worth 3000 cash. The second was square in shape, bore a horse design, and was valued at 500 cash. The third was oval in shape, bore a tortoise pattern, and had a value of 300 cash. The second and the third pieces are reported to have been reduced in weight as compared with the first one. However, since the text is apparently garbled, no exact weight is given for them. Commentators suggested that the 500 cash piece and the 300 cash piece weighed six and four ounces respectively. But if their weight was proportional to their value, the second piece should have weighed one and one-third ounce, and the third eight tenths of an ounce. The three silver pieces were demonetized in 113 B.C. and no specimens have been preserved. It has been conjectured that these silver pieces were made as a result of contact with Chinese Turkestan where silver coins were circulated. The shapes and designs, however, were undoubtedly originated from contemporary Chinese superstitions, because the three animals, dragon, horse, and tortoise, were said to represent the functions of heaven, earth, and mankind.

5.9 Gold and silver were included in the complicated currency system of Wang Mang, but circulated only by weight. One catty of gold was valued at 10,000 cash, which was the normal Han value. A superior silver produced from Shu-shih in the modern Szechwan province was valued at 1580 cash per *liu* or eight ounces. A *liu* of ordinary silver was worth only 1000 cash. The *liu* represented half a catty and may have been a common unit of silver in Han times because the largest "white metal" piece of Wu-ti also had this weight. Hence the ratio between gold and ordinary silver was 5 to 1 at the time of Wang Mang.

5.10 History records no issue of silver currency in the Latter Han dynasty. Certain specimens of silver pieces, however, bear stamped characters indicating that they were cast in this period. In the collection of a

Japanese Sinologist, there is the top part of a tablet-shaped silver bar which bears on the one side the date *Chung-yüan êrh-nien,* i.e., 57 A.D., and on the other side words which are not clear. The Imperial Museum of Japan has a whole bar of the same shape bearing the same characters mentioned above and four more indicating a government office which made it. The bar is reported to have been unearthed in the Shantung province and has a weight of 10.75 Chinese ounces.

5.11 In the collection of the American Numismatic Society there are five silver bars of the same type. They are inscribed with the words *Shang-fang tsao,* "Made in the Imperial Workshop," and *Tu-shih,* "Metropolitan Market," but bear no date. The same collection has two heavier silver pieces more or less rectangular in shape which bear an inscription which reads in part: *Chien-ho êrh-nien Shang-chün t'ing-chang chêng-chu kung-hsing,* "In the second year of Chien-ho (148 A.D.), chief of local police in the province of Shang-chün (northern part of the modern Shansi province), officially cast for general circulation." The rest of the inscription contains the names of three *yin-chiang,* "silversmiths," apparently those who cast the ingots. If the inscriptions on these silver pieces are genuine, which I am inclined to believe, they are indisputable evidence of government issuance of silver currency in the Latter Han period.

5.12 In spite of the issue of the "white metal" from 119 B.C. to 113 B.C. and possible government casting of silver pieces in the Latter Han era, gold apparently was more widely used than silver under the two Han dynasties. In the dynastic histories, there are many references to uses of gold as grants, gifts, and indicators of value in both Han periods. Similar uses of silver, however, are found only in the later part of the Latter Han era. The use of gold and silver declined in the period of the Six Dynasties when their monetary functions were largely replaced by silk, which was by far the most important medium of exchange. The two precious metals nevertheless recovered gradually after the sixth century. The recovery of silver was particularly remarkable. Coming down to the T'ang dynasty, we find silver already more widely circulated than gold.

(2) *From the T'ang Dynasty to the Ch'ing Dynasty*

5.13 Silver ingots of T'ang and Sung date have been preserved. They are specimens in *ting* of 50 ounces. A T'ang specimen is rectangular in shape and bears an incised inscription. It was a *ting* of *Tuan-wu chin-fêng-yin,* i.e., silver presented to the throne for the festival on the fifth day of the fifth moon. It was presented by Ts'ui Shên-yu, a high commissioner stationed at

Jun-chou, the modern Chenkiang, Kiangsu. Since the full title of Ts'ui is incised, a study of his biography in the T'ang history reveals that the date of the ingot's presentation was the middle of the ninth century. Incidentally, Jun-chou had an important silver mine which was reported to have produced an annual sum of over 100,000 ounces in the early part of the ninth century.

5.14   Three preserved Sung ingots bearing inscriptions were all cast in this shape: ⊐⊏ . One belongs to the American Numismatic Society, and is probably attributable to the twelfth century. Its inscription may be translated as follows: "Silver ingot, *ting*, weighing 50 ounces, commuted for corvée exemption money of the Chin-t'ang-hsien (district), Huai-an-chün (political division)." The district is in the modern Szechwan province. The commutation was from cash to silver. The two other ingots are discussed and illustrated in the *Tōa senshi*. Both were *Ta-li yin*, literally "great ceremony silver" presented to the throne. One was from Ta-chou, in modern Szechwan, and was cast for the years 1227 and 1228. The name of the acting prefect of Ta-chou and his titles are incised. Three other names seem to have been those of the silversmiths who cast the ingot. The other ingot was from a district in T'an-chou, of modern Hunan. The silver was purchased from a merchant whose name, as well as that of the magistrate, is incised. The incision of the names of the officials, silversmiths, and the merchant indicates responsibility. It is a practice followed regularly in later times.

5.15   These silver ingots are good indicators of the use of the precious metal as money. In a monumental study, the Japanese scholar Katō Shigeru has written the history of gold and silver in T'ang and Sung times, centering on their monetary use. For each dynasty, he lists the uses of the precious metals in the private and the public sectors of the economy. Gold and silver in T'ang times were used as bribes, gifts, donations, prizes, stakes in gambling, traveling expenses, means of transferring funds to distant places, indicators of value, payments for commodities, means of hoarding in private economy and as tribute, grants, and military expenses in public finance. As indicators of value and payments for commodities, the precious metals were limited to large transactions. In general, their use was confined to the upper classes.

5.16   In Sung times, the uses of precious metals even spread to the lower classes. In addition to the above uses, gold and silver were also used as indemnity payments, to make loans, to commute taxes, and to redeem paper money. Rules against forgery of gold and silver were proclaimed. The increasing importance of silver is also revealed in our specimen of the Sung ingot for the commutation of cash payment in lieu of forced labor.

5.17 This growth in monetary uses of gold and silver was made possible by increased production of the precious metals and importation of them from foreign countries to settle a favorable balance of payments. Most gold and silver mines were found in south China. Metal produced from the mines was subject to a 10–20 per cent tax in T'ang and Sung times. In addition, the government reserved the right to make purchases from the remainder of the metal produced. The silver mine tax in T'ang times yielded an annual sum of 15,000 taels around the middle of the ninth century. In Sung times the figure jumped to 200,000 to 300,000 taels in the second half of the eleventh century. Although the Sung figure seems to have included silver purchased by the government, the increase in production must have been considerable. New silver mines discovered in Fukien undoubtedly contributed a good proportion.

5.18 Foreign trade involved both import and export of gold and silver. The balance of trade with regard to the South Sea countries probably was only slightly in favor of China; gold and silver, however, were more frequently imported from Korea and Japan. As for overland relations, the Sung dynasty, because of its military weakness, made annual gifts to its neighbors in the north, the Liao dynasty, and later to the Chin dynasty. The gifts consisted of large amounts of silk and silver, usually in a few hundred thousand bolts and taels. Balances from trade with Liao and Chin on the other hand were more than enough to offset these gift payments.

5.19 Outside the "white metal" of Han Wu-ti, the only government issue of silver currency recorded in history was under the Chin dynasty. In 1197, silver pieces were cast in five weights varying from one to ten ounces. One ounce was equivalent to two strings of copper coins. These silver ingots, presumably of a standard quality, were called *Ch'êng-an pao-huo,* "precious currency of the Ch'êng-an period." The main purpose of issuing this silver currency was to back up the paper money called *yin-ch'ao,* "silver notes," which had been in circulation. This government issue was discontinued after 1200. No specimens of the *Ch'êng-an pao-huo* are known to be in existence.

5.20 The Yüan dynasty designated paper money as the sole currency of China. Since gold and silver were used as reserves, the unit *ting* of 50 taels was also used to refer to paper notes representing a *ting* of silver. Foreign trade continued to flourish along both land and sea routes. Merchants who came to China were obliged to exchange their silver for notes. This helped the government to concentrate large amounts of the precious metal in its treasury. The total amount of silver within Chinese territory probably also increased. As a result, when paper money declined in Ming and Ch'ing times, silver was adequate to function as the major form of money for large transactions. Two factors which helped this development considerably were the importation of silver from the Philippines (indirectly from Spain and Mexico) and the increased silver production in Yunnan and Burma in the sixteenth and seventeenth centuries. Foreign silver dollars and bullion were imported and circulated in the coastal provinces of Fukien and Kwangtung. A seventeenth-century book suggests that silver produced in Yunnan was more than double the amount produced in eight other provinces of China.

5.21 In the Yüan period, a *ting* generally referred to 50 ounces of silver or the same amount of paper money. Occasionally *ting* was used for ingots of lighter weight. In Ming times, a *ting* as a rule indicated only 5 ounces of silver, or 5000 copper coins, or their equivalent in paper money. This change may have resulted from the increasing use of silver as a medium of exchange in small transactions. A term which marked the increasing use of silver in the payment of taxes was *chin-hua yin,* literally "gold-patterned silver." In the early years of the Ming dynasty, commutation of tax payments into silver was permissible but not a common practice. In 1436 a decree made a considerable portion of land tax payable in silver, which was called *chin-hua yin.* The income in that year amounted to 1,000,000 ounces. As a term for fine silver, however, *chin-hua yin* already existed in the T'ang period.

5.22 In this connection, we may discuss a few terms referring to gold and silver. Most of these were in use from Sung or even earlier times. *Ma-ti chin,* "horse-hoof gold," *kua-tzŭ chin,* "melon seed gold," and *sha-chin,* "sand gold," referred to natural gold in the various forms. *Tzŭ-mo chin,* "purple polished gold," denoted gold of the finest quality, whereas ordinary gold was known as *ch'ih-chin,* "red gold." According to the Japanese scholar Katō Shigeru, the term *chung-chin* referred to gold of medium grade. I feel that it may have been used to mean silver rather than gold.

5.23 Terms for silver were even more numerous. Ordinary silver was known as *pai-yin,* "white silver." *Hua-yin,* "flower silver," and *hsüeh-hua yin,* "snow-flake silver," sometimes referred to a superior grade. The term *hsi-ssŭ wên-yin,* "fine silk pattern silver," gave rise to the famous name *sycee,* which was undoubtedly from a dialectical pronunciation of the words *hsi-*

ssŭ. The term *ma-t'i yin,* "horse-hoof silver," may have been related to the English word "shoe" referring to *sycee* silver because both terms indicated the oval shaped ingots which were generally known as *yüan-pao.* The term *yüan-pao* first appeared in 1276 when large amounts of *sa-hua yin-tzŭ* or "gift silver" (actually booty) were cast into ingots of 50 ounces each. Smaller pieces of silver were commonly known as *ping,* "cakes," in T'ang and Sung times but more frequently *k'o-tzŭ,* "ingots," in later periods.

5.24 Silver ingots in circulation were rarely of the same degree of fineness. A standard unit of account thus became necessary. Toward the end of the Ch'ing dynasty, there were three taels of currency which had a more or less national range, whereas a number of local taels served as the standard units in different areas. The three commonly known taels were the *K'u-p'ing* or "Treasury" tael, the *Ts'ao-p'ing* or "Tribute" tael, and the Haikwan or "Customs" tael. The local taels usually had their own names. For instance, the Shanghai tael was known as *Chiu-pa kuei-yüan,* "98 conventional unit," and the Tientsin tael as *Hang-p'ing hua-pao,* "Guild weight currency treasure." Like the three national taels, these were also fictitious money, used as units of account. The *Chiu-pa kuei-yüan* derived its name from the local convention of accepting 98 taels to settle a transaction of 100 taels.

5.25 Under the Ch'ing dynasty, firms which specialized in the casting of silver ingots were known as *lu-fang (loofang)* in north China and *yin-lu* in south China. They made ingots for banks at a small charge and were fully responsible for their product. In south China, before the cast ingot was circulated, it had to be examined and certified by the House of Assayance or *kung-ku (kungkoo) chü.* There was a small charge for this service. To indicate approval of the piece, the assayer would place his stamp on it or mark it with Chinese ink, giving details of its weight and fineness. In north China, where houses of assayance were few, the *lu-fang* performed this function. The *kung-ku chü* and *lu-fang* or *yin-lu* had to secure licenses from the government before beginning operations. Generally only one house of assayance and a small number of *lu-fang* or *yin-lu* would be permitted in a locality.

5.26 The exchange rate between gold and silver fluctuated from time to time. It has been pointed out that the ratio at the beginning of the Christian era was 5 to 1. Ratios from the Sung time on are listed as follows. Interpretations of these figures however have not been found in each case and have to be left to another study.

Date	Gold	Silver
977	1	8
c. 1000	1	6.3
1015	1	6.3
1126	1	13.3
1134	1	13
1209	1	12.1
1282	1	7.6
1287	1	10
1309	1	10
1375	1	4
1385	1	5
1413	1	7.5
c. 1600	1	8
1662	1	10
1700	1	10
1740	1	12.5
1750	1	14.9
1775	1	16.15
1779	1	18
1782	1	20
1840	1	18
1850	1	14
1882	1	18

(3) Foreign and Native Silver Dollars

5.27 The Spanish Carolus dollar was introduced into China via the Philippines in the sixteenth century. For many years it was the chief foreign currency accepted by the Chinese, although it circulated only by weight and primarily in the coastal provinces of Fukien and Kwangtung. In the second half of the nineteenth century, its leading position gradually passed to the Mexican dollar. At this time the silver dollar had already become a familiar feature in many Chinese cities. Other foreign dollars also circulated in competition with the Mexican dollar. These included the British Hongkong dollar (issued 1866–1868), the American trade dollar (1873–1887), the Japanese yen (1871–1897), and a few others. The Mexican dollar, however, maintained its predominance until the end of the nineteenth century.

5.28 Foreign dollars in general were known as *fan-yin*, "barbarian silver," *fan-ping*, "barbarian cake," and *yang-ch'ien*, "foreign coin." Clean and uninjured dollars were called *kuang-pan*, "clean pieces," and chopped ones *lan-pan*, "debased pieces," or *lan-fan*, "debased barbarian (silver)." Spanish dollars had the name *pên-yang*, "standard dollar," Mexican dollars *ying-yang*, "eagle dollar," and British Hongkong dollars *chan-jên yang*, "standing person dollar." The first name probably referred to the popularity of the Spanish dollar; the other two names apparently indicated the designs of the two dollars.

5.29 The Spanish dollar was also known as *shuang-chu*, "double pillar," referring to its design of Pillars of Hercules. The terms "Pillar dollar" and "Eagle dollar" were sometimes used by writers in English to indicate the Spanish and Mexican dollars. Pillar dollars made in the reign of Carolus IIII (1788–1808) were very popular in China and used to bear a premium over their intrinsic value in the nineteenth century. They were called *ssŭ-kung yin* in Chinese because the Roman numeral IIII was compared to a repetition of the Chinese character *kung* four times. Another Spanish pillar dollar, bearing the stamp of the letter G, or G^a, denoting that it was from the Guadalajara mint in Mexico, was called by the Chinese *kou-ch'ien*, "hooked dollar," from its resemblance to that letter. This coin was often received at a discount.

5.30 The circulation of foreign silver dollars in China convinced many Chinese that native coinage of similar type was desirable. In the process of imitation of foreign dollars, two different trends are noticeable. One school was in favor of a native 7.2 mace dollar, identical in weight to most foreign dollars. The other preferred a one-tael dollar in order to maintain the traditional tael unit. Experimentation with both kinds was carried out in different places. The influence of foreign trade and foreign dollars, however, was undoubtedly too strong. Toward the end of the nineteenth century, the 7.2 mace dollar was already in winning position. In 1907, the Board of Revenue made an attempt to circulate one-tael dollars as the standard currency of the nation. It failed because most provinces refused to follow. In the Republican years, the 7.2 mace dollar became the sole main coin.

5.31 Earliest specimens bearing a date are those minted by Shanghai merchants in 1856. The large ones are one tael and the small ones 5 mace by weight. The weight, the names of the shop and the coiner are shown in Chinese characters on their faces following the tradition of silver ingots.

5.32 Native dollars undoubtedly existed before 1856. A silver dollar of 7.2 mace is said to have been minted by a rebel leader in Formosa as early as 1837. Since it has the picture of the god of longevity on one side it has been known locally in Formosa as *lao-kung yin*, "the old man silver." Silver dollars equivalent to about 7 mace were minted in Changchow, Fukien, in 1864 and 1865, by military authorities. They bear the words, *Chang-chou chün-hsiang*, "For military supplies at Changchow." Silver coins, 1 tael to

1 mace by weight, known as *hsiang-yin,* "silver for military supplies," were issued in Sinkiang in the 1870's.

5.33   In 1887 the provincial authorities of Kwangtung issued dollars of 7.3 and 7.2 mace. As we would expect, the 7.3 mace ones were soon driven from the market because of their weight. The 7.2 mace dollars proved satisfactory and were gradually imitated in other provinces. Early followers were Hupeh in 1897 and Kiangnan and Anhwei in 1897. These silver dollars have the image of a curled dragon on one side and consequently have been known as *Lung-yang,* "dragon dollars."

5.34   Certain imitations of foreign dollars are referred to in Chinese texts as *hang-chuang,* "hong dollars," *Wu-chuang,* "Kiangsu dollars," *Fu-pan,* "Foochow dollars," *Hang-pan,* "Hangchow dollars," and *Kuang-pan,* "Kwangtung dollars." They seem to indicate dollars minted by merchants in the different localities. The ones issued by Shanghai merchants in 1856 may belong to this category.

5.35   The two important types of silver dollars in the Republican years were those bearing an image of Yüan Shih-k'ai and those bearing an image of Sun Yat-sen. The former were first issued in 1914 and the latter in 1933 and 1934. They are informally known as *Yüan t'ou,* "Yüan Shih-k'ai dollars," and *Sun-t'ou,* "Sun Yat-sen dollars." The Sun Yat-sen dollar is also known in English as the "Junk" dollar, because it bears on one side a design of a junk. The minting of silver dollars was brought to an end in 1935 when the policies of demonetization of silver and legalized national currency were adopted.

5.36   Subsidiary silver coins were also minted by central and local authorities. Most of those in circulation were 20-cent and 10-cent pieces issued in the first three decades of the nineteenth century. They were known colloquially as *hsiao-yang,* "small foreign-style silver coins" in contrast with *ta-yang,* "large foreign-style silver coins" or silver dollars. As a rule, the subsidiary silver coins were depreciated and were accepted as eleven to thirteen 10-cent pieces to a dollar.

VI

Paper Money to the End of the Sung Dynasty

6.1 This chapter deals with the early history of paper money, or credit currency, to the end of the Sung era. It will start with a brief discussion of the "white deerskin money" in the second century B.C., proceed to the story of "flying money" in T'ang times, offer a comprehensive account of paper money and other credit instruments in Sung China to about 1275, and finally discuss the paper notes of the Chin dynasty.

6.2 The origin of credit currency is sometimes traced to the *pai-lu-p'i-pi* or "white deerskin money" of Han Wu-ti in 120 B.C. According to history, it was a Chinese foot to the square, had embroidered edges, and was valued at 400,000 cash. Each noble who came to pay a visit to the imperial court was required to purchase a piece of this white deerskin from the government and to present it to the emperor in addition to his regular tribute. This was evidently a device to enrich the imperial purse. The white deerskin was never intended for circulation, and consequently cannot be considered as money.

6.3 Chinese histories attribute the origin of *ch'ao-pi* or paper money to the *fei-ch'ien,* "flying money," of the T'ang period. The "flying money," also known as *pien-huan,* "credit exchange," was essentially a draft to transmit funds to distant places; hence it may be considered a credit instrument but not money. The history of paper money and that of other credit instruments, however, is so closely woven together that the "flying money" forms a logical starting point for our account.

6.4 The T'ang dynasty witnessed large-scale commercial activities, of which the most spectacular was the tea trade between south China and Ch'ang-an, the T'ang capital. The tea merchants wished to transfer profits realized from the sale of tea in north China back to the tea-producing south, but found the shipment of cash both cumbersome and perilous. The same

problem of transfer faced the provincial authorities who were obliged to
send monetary tribute and gifts to the imperial court. These authorities
maintained in the capital liaison offices known as *chin-tsou yüan,* "memorial-
presenting courts," part of whose duties was to expedite presentation of these
gifts. The transfer problem was solved by the institution "flying money,"
whereby merchants deposited cash with the "memorial-presenting courts,"
in return for vouchers guaranteeing reimbursement in designated provinces.
Thereby a double transfer of cash was realized without an actual physical
transfer. Hence the picturesque name "flying money." Parties who used the
device were not limited to tea merchants and the "memorial-presenting
courts"; other merchants and officials could make similar arrangements between the two groups or within one group.

6.5 In 811, the government prohibited the use of "flying money" by
private citizens and in the following year took over the system for its own
purposes of forwarding taxes and revenues to the capital. Merchants were
allowed to deposit cash with one of the three offices of government finance
in the capital and to receive payments in the provinces. At first, the government charged a 10 per cent fee, but very quickly abandoned it and issued
drafts on a one-string-to-one-string (*ti-kuan*) basis to tempt the merchants
to use the system. The institution was copied by the Sung dynasty under
the name *pien-ch'ien,* "credit cash." In 970 the government established a
Pien-ch'ien wu or "Bureau of credit cash" which in the following century
issued drafts totaling one to three million strings per year. Private drafts,
in spite of state prohibition, still continued to be used in T'ang and Sung
times, and were also known as *pien-ch'ien* or *pien-huan.*

6.6 The first true paper currency was *chiao-tzŭ,* "exchange medium,"
which appeared in Szechwan, in the vicinity of I-chou (the modern
Ch'êng-tu) during the early part of the eleventh century. Ever since the
period of Five Dynasties, iron coin had circulated in Szechwan. Its clumsi-
ness led people to deposit iron cash in proto-banks called *kuei-fang,* "deposit houses," and to use their receipts, which were in the nature of promissory notes, in financial transactions. In the reign of Chên-tsung (998–1022),
the government recognized sixteen merchants and granted them a monopoly
on the issue of these *chiao-tzŭ* promissory notes. These merchants were called
chiao-tzŭ hu, "exchange medium households," and their shops *chiao-tzŭ p'u,*
"exchange medium shops." The notes were printed in black and red from
blocks bearing various patterns. The denomination of the note was inked
in, ordinarily one note representing one string of cash. A fee of about 3 per
cent was charged for this service. The sixteen merchants however did not

always reimburse their clients promptly and this resulted in wide protests and many legal cases.

6.7 In the year 1016, a government monopoly was proposed to replace the private monopoly. This was realized in 1023 when the government established a *Chiao-tzŭ wu*, "Bureau of exchange medium," in Ch'êng-tu. Notes were issued with a cash reserve of approximately 29 per cent. The total amount circulated from the second month in 1024 to the second month in 1025 was 1,256,340 strings, which was established as the quota for a period of circulation which was called *chieh*. Traditional accounts define a *chieh* as three years for *chiao-tzŭ*. This may have been true when *chiao-tzŭ* was in private hands. However, when taken over by the government, the notes were issued about once every other year. From 1023 to 1197 we can count 88 *chieh* or periods. At first, there were various denominations ranging from one to ten strings. Beginning at 1039 there were only two denominations of five (20 per cent of the issue) and ten strings (80 per cent), and from 1068 on two denominations of one string (60 per cent of the issue) and 500 cash (40 per cent).

6.8 In theory, the notes issued in a period should have been called in or exchanged for notes in the following period. Actually the redemption was often postponed for one period or more. An early case was in 1072, when, in addition to the issue of 1,256,340 strings of the twenty-fifth period in 1071, another 1,256,340 strings were circulated. The 1072 issue was also to belong to the twenty-fifth period, and it was used to replace notes of the twenty-third period. History records this as the first example of an issue which was double the specified amount. The fact that the second twenty-fifth issue was used to redeem the twenty-third issue indicates that the twenty-fourth issue was still in circulation. Evidently, by 1072, the rules of replacing one issue by the following and maintaining a fixed quota for each period had both been broken.

6.9 These inflationary practices were repeated from time to time under the two Sung dynasties, primarily to meet military expenditures. Record issue was reached in 1107 during the Northern Sung period when 26,852,006 strings were outstanding. In this year the name *chiao-tzŭ* was changed to *ch'ien-yin,* "money voucher," and the office *Chiao-tzŭ wu* to *Ch'ien-yin wu.* The area of circulation was extended from Szechwan to the Yellow river and Huai river valleys. By the end of the Northern Sung period the total notes in circulation may have amounted to about seventy million strings. Since the notes were backed by little reserve, their value dropped with each increased issue. This was particularly true in the case of the unredeemed earlier issues which sometimes were worth only a quarter of the new issues.

6.10　The Southern Sung dynasty again limited the *ch'ien-yin* to the Szechwan area. The note of this period has become known as *Ch'uan-yin,* "Szechwan voucher." An effort was made in 1128 to observe the quota of 1,886,340 strings which existed in 1098. An inflationary trend nevertheless set in. In the first years of the thirteenth century, the amount of circulation rose to around fifty million strings, almost doubling the figure which existed in 1107 for the same Szechwan area.

6.11　Although the *chiao-tzŭ* in Szechwan had changed its name to *ch'ien-yin,* the name *chiao-tzŭ* was applied to paper money in other parts of the Southern Sung. In 1136 an unsuccessful attempt was made to circulate *chiao-tzŭ* in the capital city of Hangchow. Beginning in 1166 *chiao-tzŭ* in denominations of one string and 200, 300, and 500 iron cash were issued for circulation along with iron coins in the Huai valley. These notes have been known as *Huai-chiao,* "exchange medium in the Huai valley." Obviously it was intended to help maintain a zone of iron cash to prevent exportation of copper. For a short period, copper coins and the *hui-tzŭ* notes, which were used in the central and lower valleys of the Yangtze river, were not allowed to cross the river to the north. After the ban was lifted, two kinds of coins (copper and iron) and two kinds of paper currency (*hui-tzŭ* and *Huai-chiao*) circulated concurrently in the Huai area.

6.12　No specimens of Sung notes are preserved. A description of ten *chiao-tzŭ,* i.e., *ch'ien-yin* notes of the seventieth to the seventy-ninth period (1161–1179), is found in a Ming work on Szechwan, which quotes a Yüan author. According to this source, the notes bore very complicated and elaborate patterns in color, undoubtedly following the tradition of the private *chiao-tzŭ.* On a note one would find: (1) the number of the period or *chieh;* (2) the year of issue; (3) a five-word phrase which was usually a proverb or maxim; (4) the word *ch'ih,* "decree," surrounded by a pattern; (5) a blue pattern of flowers or animals; (6) a red pattern of historical or legendary stories; (7) the time limit surrounded by a flower pattern; (8) a pattern of stories on the back, which was different for the one-string and 500-cash notes of the same issue; and (9) the amount issued (*shu-fang,* "to write and let go; to issue"). Except for the blue pattern and the red pattern, the note was printed, or rather, stamped, with black ink. According to the same book, similar forms were used in the Northern Sung period, and six printing seals were cast as early as 1107 to print the patterns in blue, red, and black on both sides of the note.

6.13   The paper money *par excellence* of the Southern Sung period was *hui-tzŭ*, "check medium." Like its predecessor *chiao-tzŭ*, *hui-tzŭ* also originated as a private instrument. In the middle of the twelfth century, notes by this name were issued by private monetary agencies in the area of the capital, Lin-an, the modern Hangchow. In 1160 the government prohibited the circulation of private *hui-tzŭ* and issued their own, which were sometimes designated as *kuan-hui,* "the official check medium," in order to distinguish them from the private notes. Denominations were in 1, 2, and 3 strings.

6.14   In 1168, the period of circulation or *chieh* was established at three years and the quota for each period was fixed at ten million strings. Small denominations of 200, 300, and 500 cash were added. At first, the *hui-tzŭ* circulated only around the capital, but in time they spread to neighboring provinces until their circulation reached every corner of Southern Sung China, with the exception of Szechwan. During this period the government again found in paper money an expedient means of meeting excessive expenditures. From 1176 on, certain issues were permitted to circulate for six or nine years. In 1195 the quota for a period was raised to thirty million strings. In 1209 old and new notes of three periods which were in circulation totaled about 117,600,000 strings; in 1232 notes of two periods amounted to an even larger figure, 329,000,000 strings. From 1247 on, notes of two periods were permitted to circulate without a time limit. Since these inflationary measures were taken with no regard for the market demands for currency, they brought about a rapid decline in the value of the *hui-tzŭ*.

6.15   In its first few decades, the value of *hui-tzŭ* was fairly steady. In accordance with the Sung practice of reckoning 77 cash as one hundred, a string of *hui-tzŭ* was to exchange for 770 cash. Until about 1208 the market price in the capital fluctuated around 700 cash. In the provinces it was considerably lower, approximating 600. The difference was probably due to a larger demand for paper currency and more strict government control in the capital. After about 1210, the value of *hui-tzŭ* declined markedly. By 1263 even the official rate had sunk to 250 cash. Toward the end of the dynasty, it became almost worthless.

6.16   Unlike the *chiao-tzŭ* in Szechwan which bore stamp prints of three colors, *hui-tzŭ* is reported to have been printed from single brass plates in one color. A Japanese work on numismatics of Eastern Asia reproduces the photograph of a note-printing brass plate, and suggests that it may have come from the Sung dynasty. It is 3 Chinese inches wide and 5.3 inches long. The top quarter of the plate contains a drawing of ten coins. The next quarter bears twenty-nine characters reading, "With the exception of Szechwan, this may be circulated in the various provinces and districts to make public and private payments representing 770 cash per string." The bottom half is a picture of the courtyard of a granary and three persons carrying bags of grain. Three characters at the corner of the picture read *ch'ien ssŭ ts'ang,* "May there be a thousand of such granaries," which is, of course, an allusion to a line in the *Book of Odes.* According to the Japanese author, the plate may have been used to print *hui-tzŭ.*

6.17   The example of printing from a single plate was followed in the paper currency of Chin, Yüan, and subsequent dynasties, of which specimens are preserved. The pattern of such notes is comparatively simple. When drafts, checks, and paper notes were issued by native banks from the middle of the Ch'ing dynasty, there was a revival of colorful print and elaborate design, similar to the pattern of *chiao-tzŭ* as it is described in the Ming work. The expression for a draft in the Ch'ing period, *hui-p'iao,* was undoubtedly influenced by the term *hui-tzŭ.* The modern term for a draft is *hui-p'iao,* with a different character for *hui.*

6.18   In addition to the *hui-tzŭ* of which the circulation was almost nation-wide, there were two kinds of local *hui-tzŭ* in Southern Sung China. In the year 1137, a note called *yin-hui-tzŭ* or *yin-hui,* "silver check medium," was issued by local military commanders in Shensi and Szechwan, notwithstanding objections from the court. It was issued in two denominations: one mace and half a mace. It was convertible into the local paper money *Ch'uan-yin* at the rate of 4 mace to 1 string, but apparently it was not convertible into silver. Presumably the amount issued was not large.

6.19   The other local *hui-tzŭ* was the *Hu-Kuang hui-tzŭ* or *Hu-hui,* which was circulated by the government from 1163. Its name indicates that its area of circulation was the modern Hupei and Hunan provinces. Like *Huai-chiao,* the *Hu-hui* marked a special area where a local paper money circulated along with the national *hui-tzŭ.* The *Huai-chiao* and *Hu-hui* each averaged only a few million strings at a time. Nevertheless they added to the inflation in the later part of the Southern Sung period.

6.20   Prior to the issue of the national *hui-tzŭ,* in 1159 two other notes were put into circulation in three localities. One was called *kung-chü,* "public certificates," of which 400,000 strings were issued for the area to the east of the Huai river. The other was known as *kuan-tzŭ,* "communicating medium," of which 800,000 strings were issued in Hu-Kuang (Hupei and Hunan provinces) and another 800,000 strings in the area to the west of the Huai river. The period of circulation was two years for *kung-chü* and three years for *kuan-tzŭ*. They were issued in five denominations from 10 strings to 100 strings. These eventually were replaced by the *hui-tzŭ* issued after 1160.

6.21 The large denominations of *kung-chü* and *kuan-tzŭ* indicate that the notes were not intended for ordinary commercial transactions. As a matter of fact, the notes were issued to assist in the finances of the local government since apparently they were redeemable only in the capital. These notes provided a means for the government to send funds to the provinces and for merchants to send funds to the capital. As a means of transferring payments, *kuan-tzŭ* or *hsien-ch'ien kuan-tzŭ,* "cash communicating medium," had already existed in the Northern Sung period, used by both government authorities and private individuals like the "flying money" discussed above. The Southern Sung dynasty used *kuan-tzŭ* in 1131 to supply military forces in Wu-chou (in modern Chekiang). The official quota, the fixed period of circulation, and the various denominations, however, suggest that the *kuan-tzŭ* and *kung-chü* of 1159 were similar to paper money.

6.22 Toward the end of the Southern Sung, a new note was issued in 1264 and called *hsien-ch'ien kuan-tzŭ* or *chin-yin hsien-ch'ien kuan-tzŭ,* "gold, silver, cash communicating medium." One string of the note was to be the equivalent of 770 cash or three strings of *hui-tzŭ* of the eighteenth period. Although the name sounded attractive, the note was not convertible into gold or silver or cash. Imperial decrees were issued in 1268 and 1269 prohibiting devaluation of the new note, but they were to no avail. Inflation continued until the fall of the dynasty.

6.23 In the two Sung periods, in addition to paper money like *chiao-tzŭ* and cash drafts like *pien-ch'ien,* other credit instruments called *chiao-yin* or *chiao-ch'ao,* "exchange vouchers," were in existence. These were transferable instruments, representing claims for money, salt, tea, or other commodities. These were issued by the government and handled by merchants very much like modern stocks and bonds. They had various long names but were also known by shorter general names, *ch'ao, yin,* and *ch'ao-yin,* "vouchers."

6.24 *Hsien-ch'ien chiao-yin* or "exchange vouchers for cash" were issued by the Northern Sung government for use in three border provinces, Shensi, Ho-tung, and Ho-pei. To support troops stationed in these provinces, merchants were asked to exchange money for vouchers which were redeemable in the Bureau of Government Monopolies (*Chüeh-huo wu*) in the capital. A premium was given to the merchants for encouragement. These "cash vouchers" were also known as *hsien-ch'ien chiao-ch'ao, hsien-ch'ien* *ch'ao, ch'ien-ch'ao,* and *ch'ien-yin,* the last three being abbreviations. The name *ch'ien-yin* which was given to the paper note *chiao-tzŭ* in 1107 was undoubtedly taken from names of the cash voucher.

6.25   To merchants who provided grain and fodder to armies in these provinces, the government issued *p'ing-ti liang-ts'ao chiao-yin* and *ju-chung liang-ts'ao chiao-yin.* The former represented claims for cash and the latter claims for commodities. They were convertible at the Bureau of Government Monopolies in the capital. These and the *hsien-ch'ien chiao-yin* were used primarily by the Northern Sung dynasty.

6.26   "Exchange vouchers" for salt, tea, and certain other commodities were issued by the Bureau of Government Monopolies and were redeemable in the provinces where these commodities were produced. The vouchers were known as *yen-chiao-yin, yen-chiao-ch'ao, yen-yin, yen-ch'ao,* "salt vouchers," and *ch'a-chiao-yin, ch'a-chiao-ch'ao, ch'a-yin, ch'a-ch'ao,* "tea vouchers," etc. Such vouchers often changed hands several times before they were actually presented for the commodity. These "exchange vouchers" for commodities were issued in both Northern and Southern Sung periods and served as important credit instruments in competition with paper currency.

6.27   The paper currency of the Chin dynasty was called *chiao-ch'ao,* "exchange note." It was first issued in 1153, one year after the moving of the Chin capital from Shang-ching in Manchuria to Peking. It is obvious that the institution was borrowed from Sung China and the model of *chiao-ch'ao* was *chiao-tzŭ.*

6.28   Large bills or *ta-ch'ao* were issued in denominations of 1, 2, 3, 5, and 10 strings, and small bills or *hsiao-ch'ao* in denominations of 100, 200, 300, 500, and 700 cash. The term for denomination in the Chin period was *kuan-li* or simply *li.* For instance, *êrh-kuan-li* meant the denomination of 2 strings, and *i-pai-li* that of 100 cash. Like the Sung usage, a string was not necessarily a full string. Prior to 1180, a string contained 1000 cash in government transactions but only 800 for private purposes. Beginning in that year the government also defined 800 cash as one string.

6.29   The period of circulation of *chiao-ch'ao* notes was fixed at seven years, after which old notes were retired or exchanged for new ones. The rule was observed throughout the long reign of Emperor Shih-tsung (1161–1189). When Chang-tsung came to the throne in 1189, he abolished the period of circulation. This change may be considered a step forward in the evolution of paper currency in China, because it freed the note from a time restriction. A regional restriction, i.e., a limit of note circulation within certain defined areas, however, was still in existence.

6.30 During its first few decades of circulation, the value of the *chiao-ch'ao* note was well maintained. Toward the end of the twelfth century, however, there was a tendency toward depreciation. In 1192 the Emperor decreed that the Imperial Secretariat should see to it that the amount of paper currency in circulation should not exceed that of cash. In 1193 the government ordered certain taxes which had been payable in cash in the Shensi circuit to be paid in notes. Salaries for military officers and pay to soldiers in the same circuit was to be fully or partly in notes. In 1197, notes of small denominations convertible to cash were issued in three circuits in Manchuria and these were also permitted to circulate in other provinces. Evidently notes had been circulated ordinarily only within one area and they were not always convertible to cash.

6.31 In the same year, 1197, silver ingots called *Ch'êng-an pao-huo* were cast and circulated along with the paper notes. An ounce of silver was valued at two strings of cash or paper notes. Rigid regulations were proclaimed against hoarding and exporting copper coins. Certain taxes were made payable only in silver and notes, in some cases at the prescribed ratio of half silver and half paper money. In four circuits in Manchuria transactions over one string in value were ordered to be settled with silver or notes only and not with copper coins.

6.32 The government apparently had accumulated a considerable stock of silver, which was now poured into the market to circulate along with the paper currency. Silver was undoubtedly overvalued *vis-à-vis* copper cash, because the market price in 1201 was only 80 strings of cash for a silver ingot of 50 ounces, in other words, 20 per cent lower than the official exchange of 1197. Moreover, forged *Ch'êng-an pao-huo* ingots had been discovered in the market in large quantity. They were made of silver with an alloy of much copper and tin. The people found it difficult to distinguish the genuine from the forged pieces, and the *Ch'êng-an pao-huo* was abolished in 1200. By this time, since certain taxes had been made payable in notes to the extent of 70 per cent of the total, it is apparent that paper currency still was valued.

6.33 From 1180 to 1203 a local paper currency called *san-ho-t'ung chiao-ch'ao* "three-way-checking exchange note," circulated in certain cities including Chung-tu, Nan-ching, and P'ing-liang-fu. In 1202, the government accepted this note in the payment of 10 per cent of taxes. At the beginning of 1203, after a court discussion, this local note was abolished, and the *chiao-ch'ao* note was left as the sole paper money of the Chin dynasty.

6.34 Depreciation became increasingly serious. In order to save the situation, attempts were made from 1206 to withdraw gradually the large bills. In 1207 certain taxes were required to be paid one third in large bills; later the proportion was increased to two thirds. Business transactions including mortgage and pawnbroking over a string in value were ordered to be made only in paper currency. Further regulations were issued to restrict hoarding and shipment of coins. The small notes were made convertible to coins but the amount one person could exchange from the government treasury was limited to two strings. In 1208 more taxes were made payable in notes, and the small bills were permitted to circulate without a regional limit.

6.35 These measures did not stop the trend toward inflation. Military expenses imposed too great a strain upon public finance. In 1210 before a major defeat by the Mongols, eighty-four cartloads of bills were distributed among the Chin troops. In 1214 since the old bills were practically worthless, new ones were issued in denominations from 20 to 100 strings and later from 200 to 1000 strings. In the following year the circulation of copper cash was prohibited. As a result, large amounts of coins were shipped to the Sung territory where they were highly valued.

6.36 In the same year, 1215, the *chiao-ch'ao* notes were changed to new ones called *Chên-yu pao-ch'üan*, "Precious bills of the Chên-yu era." This note established the custom of using the reign title in the name of the paper currency, a practice followed by subsequent dynasties. To maintain the value of paper notes, the government attempted price control. *Shih-ku* or "current prices" in terms of the new currency were prescribed twice a month, and these were to be observed as ceiling prices. This rule, however, was enforced only within the capital city and was officially abandoned after about two months.

6.37 In 1216, the second year of its circulation, the *Chên-yu pao-ch'üan* was already so depreciated that a note representing one string was worth only a few cash. Another paper money, *Chên-yu t'ung-pao*, "Circulating treasure of the Chên-yu era," was printed in this year and issued in 1217. The ratio between the new bill and the *Chên-yu pao-ch'üan* was established as 1 to 1000. Four strings of the new note were to be the equivalent of one ounce of silver. Five years later, in 1221, it took 800 strings of paper notes to buy one ounce of silver. A third new note was issued in 1222 under the name *Hsing-ting pao-ch'üan*, "Precious currency of the Hsing-ting era," one string being the equivalent of 400 strings of the *Chên-yu t'ung-pao* or half an ounce of silver. In 1223 two additional notes were issued; one was called *Yüan-kuang chung-pao*, "Heavy treasure of the Yüan-kuang era," and the other *Yüan-kuang chên-pao,* "Precious treasure of the Yüan-kuang era." The latter note was printed on silk.

6.38 At each of these changes, the old bills were not abolished, but continued to circulate at fantastically devalued rates. In 1223, the *Hsing-ting pao-ch'üan* was only in its second year but it was already so depreciated that the government prescribed a ratio of 300 strings to one ounce of silver. In other words, the paper note dropped to $\frac{1}{150}$ of its original value. By this time, silver had become the predominant currency. A new rule ordered that transactions under three ounces of silver were to be made entirely in paper notes and those over three ounces one third in silver and two thirds in notes. As a protest, merchants refused to open their shops even during the daytime; and the rule had to be abandoned. Thus the net result of paper currency of the Chin dynasty was an unexpected shift to silver. In 1233, one year preceding the fall of the dynasty, a note called *T'ien-hsing pao-hui,* "Precious note of the T'ien-hsing era," was issued in Ts'ai-chou, the last refuge of the Chin ruler. It was in four denominations representing one to four maces of silver. The issue apparently was an attempt to put paper money on a silver basis, but it was too late to do any good.

Paper Money from the Yüan Dynasty to the End of the Ch'ing Dynasty

7.1 The Yüan dynasty marks the climax in the evolution of early Chinese paper money. The origins of Yüan paper currency lie directly in the systems of Sung and Chin, but eventually developed far beyond them. After the Yüan, paper money declined rapidly and practically disappeared after the sixteenth century. The revival of paper currency in the nineteenth century was largely the result of the impact of economic forces from the Western world.

7.2 The earliest reference to paper notes under the Mongols is in the last years of Činggis' reign. About 1227, a military commander of Po-chou in modern Shantung printed paper currency, using silk yarns as his reserve. Since Po-chou was a district where silk was produced in quantity, this major commodity served as a convenient reserve. The note was called *hui-tzŭ,* which is the same as the main paper money of the Southern Sung dynasty.

7.3 Prior to 1260, other local authorities also issued notes in areas under their jurisdiction. These were referred to as *hsing-yung ch'ao,* "circulating notes." Most of them appear to have been circulated for a period of about three years. In general, silver was used as the reserve and the amount of notes in circulation was not large.

7.4 In 1236 and 1253, the central government issued paper money called *chiao-ch'ao,* adopting the model of Chin. The issuance, however, was not in large quantities and no immediate attempts were made to unify the various local notes. In 1236, upon the suggestion of the celebrated statesman Yeh-lü Ch'u-ts'ai, ten thousand *ting* were made the maximum amount of government issue. A *ting* was the equivalent of fifty ounces. The ratio between notes and silver is not known. Backing from the central government undoubtedly contributed to the popularity of paper notes. William of Rubruck, who was in Qaraqorum during the reign of Emperor Möngke (1251–1259) mentions the existence of paper money bearing the Emperor's seal.

7.5 Qubilai ascended the throne in 1260. The year was marked by the issuance of three new notes, of which one was destined to unify the currency system of the empire. In the seventh month, paper money called *ssŭ-ch'ao,* "silk note," was issued with silk yarns as a reserve. This was apparently an imitation of the local *hui-tzŭ* in Po-chou. According to the Yüan history, "fifty ounces of silver were made the equivalent of one thousand ounces of silk notes." The text, however, may have been garbled, and a reasonable emendation would read: "fifty ounces of silver were made the equivalent of one hundred ounces of this note and one thousand ounces of silk yarns." The "silk note" was also known as *chiao-ch'ao,* which had already assumed the general meaning of paper currency by the Yüan period.

7.6 In the same year another bill was woven out of silk and called *Chung-t'ung yin-huo,* "silver currency of the Chung-t'ung era." It was in five denominations from one to ten ounces. Although intended to represent silver in full value, it does not seem to have been actually in circulation.

7.7 In the tenth month of 1260, an epoch-making note was issued. Its full name was *Chung-t'ung yüan-pao chiao-ch'ao,* "primary treasure exchange note of the Chung-t'ung era." The name was sometimes shortened to *Chung-t'ung yüan-pao ch'ao* or simply *Chung-t'ung ch'ao.* The note had ten denominations representing 10, 20, 30, 50, 100, 200, 300, 500, 1000, and 2000 cash. Apparently it was intended to be convertible into either silver or copper, because a string of 1000 cash was established as the equivalent of one ounce in paper notes or half an ounce of silver, and the amount issued was indicated in terms of *ting,* or fifty ounces. The reserve consisted of gold and silver and particularly silver.

7.8 The note was circulated in all provinces without a time limit. Old notes of various kinds were redeemed at fair rates. In 1276, old Sung *hui-tzŭ* notes were redeemed at the rate of fifty strings of *hui-tzŭ* to one string of the Chung-t'ung note. In 1280, offices were established to circulate Chung-t'ung notes in Uighur areas. In fact, the new note had become the universal paper currency of the whole empire.

7.9 In order to maintain the value of the new currency, the government made it the sole currency by demonetizing copper, gold, and silver. Already in 1262 it forbade the use of gold and silver as media of exchange. Fractional bills called *li-ch'ao* in denominations of 2, 3, and 5 cash were issued in 1273. The coins in the Sung territory were abolished in 1280 upon the conquest of South China. Notes were convertible into gold and silver, provided the bullion was to be manufactured into utensils or ornaments. These precious metals, however, were not allowed to circulate.

7.10 For almost two decades, the Chung-t'ung note enjoyed the full confidence of the people. This was mainly due to a cautious policy adopted by the government. New notes were issued every year from 1260 but they were in small amounts and had an almost 100 per cent reserve. In 1269, the total amount in circulation was only about seven hundred thousand *ting*. The situation began to change in the late 1270's. In the single year of 1276, newly issued notes numbered more than 1.4 million *ting*. Similar amounts were added in subsequent years until a new peak was reached in 1285 and 1286 when the new issue of each year amounted to over two million *ting*. The new domains of the Mongols undoubtedly absorbed much of the currency, but inflation was already noticeable. The fractionary bills printed in 1273 were abandoned in 1278, probably because increased prices had rendered them useless.

7.11 The following seventy years from 1280 to 1350 saw a period of mild but continuous inflation. Military expeditions, court grants, and religious ceremonies all proved costly. More notes were issued while gold and silver reserves were used for other purposes. During three periods, from 1283 to 1285, 1287 to 1304, and 1309 to 1311, the government prohibited private trading of gold and silver. The two latter occasions were to promote the circulation of new paper notes issued in 1287 and 1309. The prohibition, however, was not effective enough to concentrate much precious metal in the government treasury.

7.12 In 1287 a new currency was issued in eleven denominations from five cash to two strings. The note was called *Chih-yüan t'ung-hsing pao-ch'ao,* "circulating precious note of the Chih-yüan era." Its short name was *Chih-yüan ch'ao.* An exchange rate of 1 to 5 was established between the Chih-yüan and the Chung-t'ung notes. The old notes remained in circulation. The exchange rate gives an indication of the rise of prices which had developed since 1260.

7.13 In 1309 another new note was issued. It was called *Chih-ta yin-ch'ao,* "silver note of the Chih-ta era." There were ten denominations from two *li* (one-thousandth of an ounce) to two ounces. An exchange rate of 1 to 5 was established between the Chih-ta and the Chih-yüan bills. This proved to be too strong an inflationary force, and the silver note was abolished after a year and eight months.

7.14 From 1311 on, the Chung-t'ung and Chih-yüan notes were proclaimed the only legal money and both continued to be printed from year to year. The ban on trading in gold and silver was also lifted. Prices fluctuated from period to period, but the mild inflation never stopped.

7.15 The year 1350 marked the last currency reform of the Yüan and the beginning of malignant inflation. A new currency called *Chung-t'ung chiao-ch'ao*, "exchange note of the Chung-t'ung era," was issued to circulate at the rate of 1 to 2 Chih-yüan notes. To distinguish it from the old Chung-t'ung note which was first issued in Qubilai's reign, it was also called *Chih-chêng* note. Copper coins were also revived and one thousand cash were made the equivalent of one string of this new Chung-t'ung or Chih-chêng note.

7.16 Three kinds of paper money, Chung-t'ung, Chih-yüan, and Chih-chêng, were circulated along with copper coins, but the people valued only the hard cash. Rebellions spread over the whole empire. To meet increasing financial needs, new notes were issued in huge amounts without any reserve. After about 1356, paper money had practically no value and the people resorted to copper coins or exchange by barter until the end of the dynasty in 1368.

7.17 In its heyday, the Yüan paper currency circulated not only in Chinese and Uighur areas but also penetrated to Burma, Siam, and Annam. It was also introduced into Persia, where the Mongols ruled for many years. There paper money was known as *čau* from the Chinese *ch'ao* and reckoned in *balīš*, "pillow," similar to a *ting*. Together with paper notes, Chinese banking practices became known to the West. Max Weber states that the accounting system (Verrechnungswesen) of the old Hamburg Bank was set up on a Chinese model. Robert Eisler suggests that the old Swedish system of banking and money deposit vouchers may have been influenced by Chinese examples, transmitted by medieval merchant-travelers and, possibly, by Jewish silk merchants.

7.18 Since paper money reached a high point under the Yüan dynasty, it seems appropriate to discuss some general terms at the end of the account of the notes of this period. Regulations regarding paper currency were particularly elaborate in the Yüan period. Many details are preserved in the *Yüan tien-chang*, a collection of Yüan statutes, which contains sections on *hun-ch'ao*, "illegible notes," *wei-ch'ao*, "counterfeit notes," and *t'iao-ch'ao* "pieced-together notes."

7.19 The illegible notes were usable as long as the figures indicating the value (*kuan-pai*) were legible. Notes which were illegible and ragged (*hun-lan*) could be exchanged for new ones. For the exchange, the government charged a fee for the expense of printing the notes (*kung-mo ch'ien*, "labor and ink money") which was 3 per cent of the value of the note in 1265 and 2 per cent in 1266. These rules, however, were by no means innovations of the Yüan dynasty. A similar 3 per cent printing charge had been made by the Sung dynasty on the note *chiao-tzŭ*. The *kung-mo ch'ien* of Chin notes was 1.5 per cent in 1154, 0.8 per cent in 1183, and 1.2 in 1197.

7.20 Exchange of old notes or *lao-ch'ao* for new ones, and that of notes for metallic money and vice versa were all known as *tao-huan*. Precise definitions were given to *lao-ch'ao* and as many as twenty-five criteria were indicated in 1298. Careful regulations were issued as to how old bills were to be destroyed in the presence of the public, because corrupt practices such as destruction of counterfeit notes in lieu of genuine ones actually existed.

7.21 The right of printing notes was reserved for the government. Special offices were established for the administration of paper currency, for instance, the *Chiao-tzŭ wu* of the Sung, the *Chiao-ch'ao k'u* of the Chin, and the *P'ing-chun hsing-yung k'u* of the Yüan dynasty. One exception to the government monopoly on paper notes was in the last decades of the thirteenth century when the Yüan dynasty permitted two expirate admirals to print their own notes as a reward for their services in the transportation of tribute grain via sea routes. This privilege was granted about 1286 but revoked in 1303 when the two admirals lost imperial favor.

7.22 Counterfeiting of paper currency was subject to severe penalties. Under the Sung dynasty the penalty seems to have been limited to exile. In the Chin and Yüan periods, it was capital punishment. This was followed in theory by the Ming and Ch'ing dynasties when paper money had declined. Those who brought counterfeiting to the attention of the authorities were as a rule rewarded. One form of counterfeiting was to paste together bits of notes, so that one ounce became two ounces, etc. Such notes were called *t'iao-ch'ao* and the practice was subject to a penalty lighter than that for counterfeit printing.

7.23 Maintenance of the value of paper currency at a certain level was called *ch'êng-t'i*, a term which first appeared in Sung times. This was effected either by keeping a reserve in cash or precious metals, which was known as *i-ch'ien ch'êng-t'i*, "to maintain with cash," or by enforcing an official rate of exchange between cash and notes, and between old and new notes, which was known as *i-fa ch'êng-t'i*, "to maintain with law." The most effective way of maintenance with law was, of course, acceptance of paper notes in tax payments.

7.24 A few years after the reunification of China by the Ming dynasty, its founder, T'ai-tsu, attempted a revival of paper currency. In 1374 a *Pao-*

ch'ao t'i-chü-ssŭ, or "Precious note control bureau," was established and in the following year a note called *Ta-Ming pao-ch'ao,* "Precious note of the Great Ming," was issued. T'ai-tsu's reign title, Hung-wu, appeared on the note. In honor of the founder of the dynasty, notes printed in later reigns also bore the same reign title, although the other Ming emperors had their own reign titles.

7.25 The note was issued in six denominations, namely, 100, 200, 300, 400, 500 cash and one string. One string in paper currency was made the equivalent of 1000 copper coins, one ounce of silver, or one-fourth ounce of gold. Trading with gold and silver was forbidden. Commercial taxes were ordered to be paid 30 per cent in cash and 70 per cent in notes. In 1385 salary rice for officials was ordered to be converted into notes. In 1389 fractional notes from 5 to 30 cash were printed to facilitate small transactions.

7.26 From the very beginning the Ming note was inconvertible. Copper coins circulated along with paper currency, and the prohibition of the use of gold and silver as media of exchange was repeated but not enforced. The exchange value of notes declined rapidly and measures had to be taken to maintain it. In 1393 the government temporarily forbade the use of copper coins. In 1404 it decreed that a salt tax should be paid in notes in order to draw off the excess currency. In 1429 twelve regional customs stations called *ch'ao-kuan* were established to collect inland transit duties in paper currency. These devices, however, proved to be of little avail. One ounce of silver which was officially worth one string in notes in 1375, was valued at 35 strings toward the end of the fourteenth century, at 80 strings in the first quarter of the fifteenth century, and over 1000 strings by the middle of the century. Instead of paper currency, silver had become the major medium of exchange. The note practically ceased in circulation from the sixteenth century. The government only belatedly announced payments in silver for official salaries and transit duties.

7.27 The advantages of a paper currency, however, were not forgotten. This is illustrated by a proposal to revive it in the year 1643 when the dynasty was approaching its end. As many as ten advantages were listed in a memorial which pleased the Emperor greatly. "The first was that it could be manufactured at a low cost. The second was that it could circulate widely. The third was that it could be carried with ease, being light. The fourth was that it could be readily kept in concealment. The fifth was that it was not liable to division like silver into different grades of purity. The sixth was that it did not need weighing whenever it was used in a commercial transaction as was the case with silver. The seventh advantage was that silversmiths could not

clip it for their own nefarious profit. The eighth was that it was not exposed
to the peering gaze of the thief's rapacity. The ninth was that if paper took
the place of copper, and copper ceased to be used for making cash, there
would be a saving in the cost of this metal to the government, or the copper
saved could be used in manufacturing arms for the troops. The tenth advantage would be that if paper were used instead of silver, the silver might
be stored up by the government." The proposal, however, was not carried
out, because the government was too weak to derive benefits from paper currency.

7.28 Silver ingots and copper cash continued to serve as the two
major forms of currency in the seventeenth and eighteenth centuries. The
Ch'ing dynasty, which succeeded the Ming, refrained from copying on any
large scale the unworthy example of Ming notes. The only early exception
was in 1650 when the government printed paper notes in the modest amount
of 128,000 strings. This was an emergency measure. The same annual quota
was maintained until 1661 when paper currency was abolished.

7.29 In 1853 the government found itself in dire need of revenue to
suppress the T'ai-p'ing rebels. It resorted to the printing of notes called
kuan-p'iao, "government bills," and *pao-ch'ao,* "precious notes." The former,
based on silver, was also called *yin-p'iao,* "silver bills," and the latter, to
represent copper cash, was also known as *ch'ien-p'iao,* "cash bills." The silver
bills were in five denominations of 1, 3, 5, 10, and 50 taels, and the cash bills
in four denominations of 500, 1000, 1500, and 2000 cash. The rate of exchange was established at one tael of silver (either notes or bullion) to two
thousand cash (either copper itself or notes). The government allowed the
people to pay part of their taxes in notes. However, since the notes were
not convertible, their value dropped rapidly. By 1861, they were accepted at
only about 3 per cent of their legal value, and soon after ceased to circulate.

7.30 In this period of struggle against the T'ai-p'ing, provincial governments in South China occasionally issued promissory notes for circulation.
The notes were to be redeemed from year to year and consequently represented short-term loans. Since they were issued from the office of the provincial treasurer or *Pu-chêng-shih ssŭ,* they were known as *ssŭ-p'iao;* and
since they were used primarily to pay soldiers and officers, they were also
known as *hsiang-p'iao.* The government often failed to cash these notes
when they matured and as a result their value depreciated sometimes to as
low as 4 per cent of their face value.

7.31 The examples in the middle of the seventeenth and nineteenth
centuries were the only notable attempts made by the government to issue

paper notes in traditional forms. Native banks in cities and towns, however, also issued notes of their own which circulated in the respective localities. These were either *yin-p'iao,* "silver bills," or *ch'ien-p'iao,* "cash bills," the same names as those issued by the government after 1853. As a matter of fact the names were applied first to private notes and later to government notes. Most references to private bank notes came from the nineteenth century, but credit instruments, at least drafts known as *hui-p'iao,* undoubtedly existed also in the seventeenth century if not in an earlier period.

7.32 Following is a description of the elaborate form of credit instruments in the nineteenth century and early twentieth century by a contemporary authority: "The bills of the Chinese banks present a neat appearance and have various devices to prevent successful counterfeiting. The wealthy banks use solid blocks of brass for engraving purposes, while the poorer banks use blocks of wood, the value of a bill and date of issue are filled in with a pen, and one or more words to facilitate the detection of a counterfeit. Various stamps, large or small, round or square, or oblong, some of which are very curiously and elaborately engraved, are impressed on different parts of the bill, using red or black ink. The right hand margin is made an inch or more wider than the left hand margin, and the use made of the wider margin is the greatest security against counterfeiting, for on the wider margin are written various words, phrases, or sentences before the bill is cut or trimmed and put in circulation, and these stamped or written sentences or phrases are cut through by a sharp knife, leaving the right hand margin about the same width as the left, though presenting a very different appearance."

7.33 Silver-casting firms known as *lu-fang* in north China occasionally issued promissory notes which circulated like bank notes in the locality. A famous case was the silver notes called *yin-fei* in Ying-k'ou, Liao-ning (Fengtien). These were issued in different denominations by the local *lu-fang* on their own credit. They were redeemable at the beginning of the third, sixth, ninth, and twelfth months, in other words, at the end of every circulation period, but not during the period. Around 1900, the amount of circulation during each period was over twenty million taels. After local bank runs in 1913 and 1919, the total issue for a period was reduced to about two million taels.

7.34 Not only native banks of different size and nature issued notes; many other business firms also did the same thing on a smaller scale. This was particularly common with creditable grocery stores. Their notes, however, were accepted only within a small area of the city. Sometimes the circulation was limited to the street on which the firm was located; consequently the notes had the nickname *chieh-t'ieh-tzŭ,* "street notes.'

7.35 Modern bank notes were first issued by foreign banks in China in the latter part of the nineteenth century. From 1866 the Hongkong and Shanghai Banking Corporation took the lead. Banks of other nations followed the practice. The earliest Chinese imitator was the first commercial bank, *Chung-kuo t'ung-shang yin-hang,* which issued notes in 1899. The central bank *Hu-pu yin-hang* began to print notes in 1906. These notes, foreign and Chinese, represented either dollars or taels. Local government banks called *kuan-yin-hao* or *kuan ch'ien-chü* also circulated notes in their provinces. These tended to represent copper cash or the modern copper coin *t'ung-yüan.* Thus different sorts of notes were issued by different kinds of banks, traditional and modern, foreign and Chinese, government and private. The result was a very confused picture, and many notes were accepted only in one locality. Regulations aiming at a centralized issue were proclaimed in 1909, but chaos in the first decades of the twentieth century made it impossible to carry out any policy of centralization. It was only in 1935 that the government began to unify successfully the system of currency. From November 4 of that year, notes issued by three government banks, namely the Central Bank, the Bank of China, and the Bank of Communications, were designated as *fa-pi* or legal tender. The privilege of note issue by other banks was revoked and their notes were withdrawn and replaced by legal notes.

VIII

Traditional Credit Institutions

(1) Pawnshops

8.1 The oldest credit institution in China is the pawnshop. Its origin is traceable to the middle of the Six Dynasties when Buddhist monasteries practiced pawnbroking with the large amount of donated wealth in their treasuries. The credit was extended to the rich as well as to the poor. History reports that in the last decades of the fifth century a humble scholar pawned a bolt of hemp cloth in a monastery treasury and a prime minister pawned a valuable fur cushion, which had been a present from the Emperor. Pledges also included the precious metal gold and livestock like the yellow cow. Apparently articles accepted for pawnbroking were of a wide variety.

8.2 Pawnshops in monasteries flourished in T'ang, Sung, and Yüan times. This was partly because they were occasionally exempted from the payment of certain taxes. Pawnshops owned and operated by laymen are reported to have existed in the T'ang period but they did not enjoy this tax exemption privilege. In the Ming and Ch'ing times when Buddhism declined, pawnbroking practically ceased to exist in monasteries, but it became a regular business for the lay society. The term *ch'ang-shêng k'u,* "long-life treasuries," in Sung and earlier times originally meant monastery treasuries with or without reference to their pawnbroking function. From the Ming period on, it has become a literary expression for pawnshops in general.

8.3 A common term used for pawnshops in T'ang and later times was *chih-k'u.* Pawnshops were also known as *chi-fu p'u* in the T'ang period, *ti-tang k'u* in Sung, and *chieh-tien k'u* in Yüan. The term *chieh-tien k'u* was so popular that its transliteration is found in the Mongolian texts of Yüan decrees. The two terms regularly employed in the Ming and Ch'ing periods were *tang-p'u* and *tien-tang.*

8.4 Pawnshops in the Ch'ing period were required to register with the government and to pay a license fee or tax. They were classified into *tien, tang, chih,* and *ya,* according to their capital, customary rates of interest, terms allowed for redemption, and amount of tax paid. *Tien* was the largest establishment and *ya* the most modest business. However, the four classes were not always clearly distinguished. For instance, in the Kwangtung province, there were three types of pawnshops, *tang-tien, an-tien,* and *ya-tien.* A *ya-tien* paid the largest amount of tax and a *tang-tien* the smallest. The usage of *tang* and *ya* was thus in opposition to the general practice. *An-tien* was the medium type in Kwangtung. The local expression *an* for pawnshops was also found in Fukien.

8.5   In addition to these main classes, there were agents called *tai-tang* or *tai-pu.* They obtained funds from pawnshops to which they handed over pledges for safe custody. Sometimes they kept the articles pledged and carried on business under the supervision of their principals. These agents were normally found in villages and small towns. Since these agents were permitted to charge a higher interest rate, to allow a shorter period of redemption and to pay only a small amount of tax or no tax at all, occasionally pawnshops of considerable size attempted to call themselves *tai-tang* or *tai-pu* in order to evade taxation. The government, however, kept a close watch for such evasion.

8.6   The premises of a pawnshop were generally surrounded by a solid, high brick wall, as a protection against fire and robbery. On the outside of the shop, there was usually written a huge character *tang,* which could be seen from a considerable distance. An important exception to this rule was in Peking, where the character was omitted, but two strings of imitation cash of large size were hung in front of the gate as a shop sign. Inside the gate there was normally a big screen so that people who came to make transactions would not be seen from the street. As a measure of precaution against robbery, counters in a pawnshop were generally several feet high.

8.7   When the pledge was accepted, a *tang-p'iao* or pawn ticket was issued to the pledger. It was a printed form bearing the date, the pledger's surname, the article, the loan, and the interest charge. The characters were often in a very cursive style which was beyond ordinary recognition. To prevent possible dispute at the time of redemption, depreciating adjectives were added freely to the description of the pledge. For instance, words like "worn out" and "badly soiled" were regularly used for clothes and furs in perfectly good conditions.

8.8   Rates of interest, as fixed by regulations promulgated by various local governments, generally did not exceed 3 per cent in the Ch'ing period. As a measure of charity, some pawnshops reduced their interest rates in the month immediately preceding the Chinese New Year. In this period, pawn tickets bearing a high rate of interest could also be renewed at a lower rate with the payment of the interest to date. This was known as *chuan-li,* "changing the interest." The terms of redemption varied from six months to three years. Toward the end of the Ch'ing dynasty, there was a tendency toward shortening the term of redemption. In the early years of the Republic, the general practice was to allow a maximum of twelve months. Unredeemed articles were periodically removed from storage and sold at auction. This was called *hsia-chia,* "to remove from the shelves," and *ta-tang,* "to get rid of pawned articles."

8.9 The staff of a pawnshop consisted of several successive grades. On the top was the manager known as *ching-li* or *kuan-shih,* who was entrusted with the over-all management by the owner or owners. Although an employee, he enjoyed full power and assumed full responsibility. Under him were external and internal officers. The external officers were called *shou-kuei,* "the first counterman," *êrh-kuei,* "the second counterman," and so on, and this group was responsible for appraising. The internal officers included the keeper of the "clothing" store, keeper of the "jewelry" store, keeper of accounts, and the cashier. Sometimes the last two officers were combined into one. Under these officers were assistant clerks and apprentices. The first counterman was sometimes known by the honorary name *ch'ao-fêng* (literally, a wealthy person, who was permitted to pay court visits). The same term was also used to refer to any senior officer of a pawnshop.

8.10 Pawnshop employees were paid partly on a monthly basis and partly on a profit-sharing basis. Their regular salaries were inadequate, but they were increased by an annual bonus. As agreed between the employer or employers and the employees, approximately 20 to 40 per cent of the year's net profit was set aside to be distributed as a bonus among the staff. The manager and the senior officers, because of their responsibility and the nature of their work, always received the lion's share. A small proportion went to the assistant clerks and the apprentices. Independent management and profit-sharing were two strong points in the organization of pawnshops which were copied by Shansi banks.

8.11 Pawnbroking was one of the most profitable businesses in the Ch'ing period. The eighteenth century and the first half of the nineteenth century saw a spectacular growth of pawnshops all over the empire. According to figures from government statutes, there were 7685 pawnshops in 1685, 9904 in 1723, 18,969 in 1753, and 23,139 in 1812. Although the figures did not cover the same number of provinces, the trend of growth is unmistakable. The development was largely the result of a long period of peace and prosperity. But it seems also to have been related to the common practice of entrusting public funds to pawnshops for investment. This practice will be discussed in another chapter.

8.12　In the middle of the eighteenth century, pawnshops almost functioned as commercial banks because they made loans on commodities like grain, silk, and cotton. Certain hoarders of rice even utilized loans thus acquired to double or redouble their speculation. For instance, with 1000 taels of silver, one could purchase a number of bushels of rice. Pawning the rice for seven or eight hundred taels, one could use the sum to purchase more rice. This process might be repeated four or five times. As a result, one could hoard rice worth four or five thousand taels with his original capital of one thousand taels. This would yield a considerable profit, especially when there was an understanding between the hoarder and the pawn-broker and when the interest rate charged by the latter was relatively low. This practice, called *t'un-tang,* "pawn hoarding," was particularly common in the provinces of Kiangsu, Chekiang, and Anhwei. To stop such hoarding for speculation, the government limited loans based on grain security to small amounts.

8.13　Pawning of grain existed already in the seventeenth century, if not in earlier times. Farmers found it convenient to pawn their surplus grain instead of selling it, because as a rule the price of grain was low when they had any for sale but considerably higher when it was necessary for them to purchase it. Pawning the grain would help them to avoid suffering from price fluctuation. Consequently the government was in favor of the practice as long as it was done on a small scale and did not lead to speculation.

8.14　From the second half of the nineteenth century and especially after the T'ai-p'ing rebellion, pawnshops reached a period of decline. This partly resulted from the unsteady political situation, but more basically from the strong competition in loan-making which came from traditional and modern banks. Since these banks relied largely on the personal credit of their customers and rarely required collateral, people of social standing naturally turned to banks instead of pawnshops for a loan. Consequently large pawnshops suffered even more than the small ones. Another factor was that pawnshops found it very difficult to weather a period of inflation because the pledges would soon be redeemed with depreciated currency. This was what happened in 1927 when the government in Hankow ordered a centralization of silver dollars. Many pawnshops in that area sustained heavy losses and went bankrupt. In the early 1930's pawnbroking recovered slightly in large cities like Shanghai, apparently because they met the needs of factory workers and city paupers.

(2) *Mutual Financing Associations*

8.15 Mutual financing associations or *ho-hui* included coöperative loan societies and similar organizations to encourage joint savings and to provide mutual help for weddings, funerals, travel, or for productive purposes. As an important means for people of the middle and lower classes to raise liquid funds, they were particularly popular in the Ch'ing period. Their history, however, can be traced back to the middle of the T'ang dynasty.

8.16 Old manuscripts discovered in Tun-huang reveal that in the T'ang period, there were social and religious clubs known as *shê* or *shê-i* attached to Buddhist monasteries. The main function of these clubs was to finance activities to promote the Buddhist religion. In a number of cases, however, social and economic functions were also performed. For instance, contributions were made jointly to fellow members to help them pay for a funeral or for travel. This kind of mutual insurance was known as *chui-hsiung chu-chi,* "to follow up when there is a happy or unhappy event." Many circulars from club officers, known as *shê-ssǔ chuan-t'ieh,* to call meetings or to ask for contributions have been preserved. According to the estimate of a modern scholar, in the ninth and tenth centuries there were usually ten to fifteen social and religious clubs attached to one monastery and the membership of each club averaged from twenty-five to forty people.

8.17 The word *shê* in very ancient times was used to mean the god of the soil or his shrine. From Han times on, *shê* acquired the meaning of social and religious clubs. Clubs to pay communal worship to deities and to promote social welfare existed in practically every district in imperial China. The noteworthy aspect of the social and religious clubs of the T'ang period was their mutual financing character.

8.18 In the T'ang period, mutual financing associations also existed outside of monasteries and were nonreligious in nature. For instance, according to history, the people in the prefecture Yung-chou (in modern Hunan province) were poor and used only man power in plowing. Wei Chou, who was the prefect c. 850, organized them into twenty *shê* or clubs. Each household was to contribute a certain sum per month to its club.

The person whose lot was drawn had the first opportunity to use the fund to buy a cow. After a long period, there was no shortage of cattle. This was an example of mutual financing through joint savings.

8.19 A famous famine relief organization which may have been related to the mutual financing associations was the *shê-ts'ang* or "club granary" introduced by the great philosopher Chu Hsi (1130–1200). It was originated in the district Ch'ung-an in modern Fukien when six hundred *shih* of government grain were granted from the ever-normal granary in the prefecture as relief loans to the people in the summer of 1168. The harvest of that winter was successful and the people were able to repay the loans in full. The grain, however, was not immediately returned to the ever-normal granary but was kept for more than a dozen years in the district to be loaned in the summer and collected in the winter with a 20 per cent interest for the period. The interest was reduced by 50 per cent in years of slight famine and canceled completely in years of serious famine. As a result, the grain which had been accumulated by 1181, after repaying the original six hundred *shih*, amounted to 3100 *shih* stored in three granaries, which had been built with funds from the grain interest. These 3100 *shih* made up the permanent fund of the "club granary." After that year loans were made at the reduced rate of 3 per cent per period.

8.20 Although the project was under government supervision, the management was in the hands of village elders, local literati, and retired officials at home. Consequently the organization was called "club granary" to indicate its semi-independent nature. Upon the request of Chu Hsi in 1181, the Emperor issued an edict encouraging the various districts to follow this successful precedent. Thereupon, a number of club granaries were organized in places in modern Chekiang and Kiangsi. In most cases, the initial capital was granted from government granaries. But in several places, generous officials also contributed grain from their own households.

8.21 The idea of the "club granary" was not entirely original on the part of Chu Hsi. It was derived from the ever-normal granary of Han and the *i-ts'ang* or "communal granary" of Sui and T'ang times. The ever-normal granary was entirely under government management. The "communal granary" was built on the basis of compulsory saving in the form of a surtax. The grain collected and stored in the granary was intended only for famine relief. The government, however, from time to time, used it for its own expenditure as if it were tax grain. The characteristic of the "club granary" was its emphasis on an independent management to avoid government interference. In this sense it was similar to a mutual financing association. Printed bylaws of the coöperative loan society in the Ch'ing period sometimes contain the phrase *Hsin-an ku-shih,* "[in accordance with] the old method of Hsin-an." Perhaps this was an allusion to the "club granary" because Hsin-an was an old name for the native place of Chu Hsi in modern Anhwei province.

8.22 The coöperative loan society toward the end of the nineteenth century is well described by A. H. Smith in his *Village Life in China:* "The simplest of the many plans by which mutual loans are effected, is the contribution of a definite sum by each of the members of the society in rotation to some other one of their number. When all the rest have paid their assessment to the last man on the list, each one will receive back all he put in and no more. The association is called in some places the 'Clubs of the Seven Worthies' (*Ch'i-hsien hui*). The technical name for any association of the kind in which coöperation is most conspicuous, is *Shê.* The man who is in need of money (*Shê-chu*) invites some of his friends to coöperate with him, and in turn to invite some of their friends to do the same. When the requisite number has been secured, the members (*Shê-yu*) assemble and fix the order in which each shall have the use of the common fund. This would probably be decided by lot."

8.23 In many such associations the use of the fund involved the payment of interest. "In societies where the rate of interest is fixed, the only thing to be decided by lot, or by throwing of dice, will be the order in which the members draw out the common fund. . . . But, if, as often happens, the interest is left open to competition, this competition may take place by a kind of auction, each one announcing orally what he is willing to pay for the use of the capital for one term, the highest bidder taking the precedence, but [ordinarily] no member ever has a second turn."

8.24 The coöperative loan society was known by various names in different places. In general, we can differentiate three types of organizations. The first was *lun-hui,* "rotating society," in which the order of rotation was fixed by agreement during the organization meeting. The second was *yao-hui,* "dice-shaking society," in which the person to use the fund was to be decided by lot or by the casting of dice (usually by shaking the dice in a prescribed manner in a jar or bowl) at each meeting. The third was *piao-hui,* "auction society," in which the fund went to the person who was willing to offer the highest interest rate. The assessment paid by the members at each meeting was not always the same. In many cases, larger assessments were required from those who used the fund first in order to compensate those who used it later.

8.25 The history of the coöperative loan society in pre-Ch'ing times is not clear. A theory about its origin, which was current in Kiangsu and Anhwei provinces, was that the organization was an invention of the *Chulin ch'i-hsien* or Seven Worthies in the Bamboo Grove in the third century. This is apparently an unreliable conjecture based on a literal interpretation of the term *Ch'i-hsien hui* mentioned above, in which the phrase *Ch'i-hsien* merely indicates seven members. Another theory, which was popular in Kwangtung, attributed the beginning of the institution to a certain P'ang Kung. The identification of the man, however, is uncertain. Probably it referred to P'ang Yün (who was also known as P'ang Chü-shih), a famous Buddhist of the ninth century. According to a tradition preserved in the Yüan drama, when he became enlightened with Buddhist teaching, he excused his debtors from the burden of repayment. There is, however, no record about his introducing any coöperative loan society. The attribution of the innovation to him perhaps represents a confused memory of the monasterial origin of mutual financing associations.

8.26 In addition to the coöperative loan society, two other types of mutual financing associations existed in the Ch'ing period and the early years of the Republic. One was to provide for funeral expenses for one's parents. This was known by names like *ch'ang-shou hui,* "long-life society," *pai-p'ao hui,* "white gown (i.e., mourning dress) society," and *lao-jên hui,* "old people's society." Members of the society promised to contribute a definite amount to a fellow member who lost a parent. Sometimes a club fund was set up for such emergencies, and the fund might be invested for interest. The other type was the joint saving organization known as *tsan-ch'ien hui,* "savings society," *tui-chin hui,* "gold-accumulating society," and so forth. It was formed by people of little means to encourage savings for investment. In the first decades of the Republic, some such "savings societies" and "gold-accumulating societies" were organized on a joint-stock basis, but their period of operation was usually limited to three years.

(3) Proto-banks

8.27 A history of Chinese banking must include two types of shops mentioned in T'ang records. These are the *kuei-fang,* or deposit shops, and the *chin-yin p'u,* or gold and silver shops. The business of the two kinds of shops was quite distinct, but both types engaged in characteristic banking activities. References to such proto-banks in T'ang and Sung sources have been collected by the Japanese scholar Katō Shigeru.

8.28 The *kuei-fang,* also known as *chiu-kuei,* dated from the middle T'ang. These shops accepted cash, gold, and silver for deposit, and unlike pawnshops, they charged the depositor a fee for the safekeeping of his valuables. The *kuei-fang* acted as custodians only, and apparently did not make loans or invest their deposits elsewhere for profit. They did honor and pay checks, called *t'ieh,* written by their depositors, and also acted as agent in the sale of entrusted goods on commission from the owner.

8.29 *Kuei-fang* are not mentioned after the Yüan, but an important Sung development, the *chiao-tzŭ p'u,* probably arose from them. The *kuei-fang* issued deposit certificates to their customers at the time of deposit, and these certificates gradually began to circulate like money. The Sung paper note *chiao-tzŭ* was originally a promissory note issued by private merchants in Szechwan toward the end of the tenth century. The note-issuing shops were known as *chiao-tzŭ p'u,* of which several appear to have been former *kuei-fang.*

8.30 The increasing use of gold and silver from the T'ang period created shops dealing with these precious metals. A *chin-yin hang,* or guild of gold and silver shops, was reported in Soochow in the middle of the ninth century, and there were also shops in Ch'ang-an in T'ang times. During the Sung they existed in the capitals of Pien-liang and Hangchow and in other important towns. A district containing more than one hundred of these shops was reported in Hangchow. The chief business of these shops was the buying and selling of gold and silver implements and ornaments, but they also dealt in gold and silver bullion, gold dust, and perhaps also in mercury and other precious objects. They made appraisals of gold and silver and employed artisans to make gold and silver objects. Those which specialized only in one of the two precious metals were known by such names as *chin-ssŭ, chin-p'u,* "gold shops," *yin-p'u,* "silver shops," and *yin-chiang p'u,* "shops of silver artisans."

8.31 Another primitive function of the banking business was added in the Sung, and especially during the Southern Sung period, when the shops began trading in salt and tea vouchers (*ch'ao-yin*). The shops bought and sold vouchers for tea, salt, and sometimes alum, in exchange for cash, which they kept on hand for sale, just as they did gold and silver. Thus they acquired longer names like *chin-yin chiao-yin p'u,* "gold, silver, and voucher shops," and *chin-yin ch'a-yen chiao-yin p'u,* "gold, silver, and tea and salt voucher shops." Those which dealt primarily with such vouchers were called *chiao-yin p'u,* "voucher shops."

8.32 These gold, silver, and voucher shops may also have dealt in forms of paper currency such as *chiao-tzŭ* and *hui-tzŭ,* but paper currency exchange does not appear to have been their chief business. In the Southern Sung period, there existed exchange shops called *tui-fang* or *tui-pien-chih-p'u.* They were small firms which specialized in the buying, selling, and exchange of silver, copper cash, and paper money.

8.33 The terms *chin-p'u* and *yin-p'u,* gold and silver shops, appeared also in Ming and Ch'ing times. A tendency toward specialization of function is revealed by the different names given to them. Shops specializing in the buying, selling, and making of gold and silver objects were called *ta-chin p'u,* "gold-manufacturing shops," and *ta-yin p'u,* "silver-manufacturing shops," in Ming times, and known as *chin-tien,* "gold stores," and *yin-lou,* "silver stores," in both Ming and Ch'ing times. Shops specializing in the casting of silver ingots were called *ch'ing-hsiao yin-p'u,* "silver-casting shops," in the Ming period and *yin-lu* or *lu-fang* in the Ch'ing period.

8.34 *Lu-fang* (*loofang*) was the term used in North China and *yin-lu* in South China. These firms made ingots for their customers at a small charge and were fully responsible for their product. In South China before the cast ingot was circulated, it had to be examined and certified by the *kung-ku* (*kungkoo*) *chü* or house of assayance. There was also a small charge for this service. To approve the piece, the assayer would place his stamp on it or mark it with Chinese ink, giving details of the weight and fineness. In North China where houses of assayance were few, the *lu-fang* also performed this function. The *kung-ku chü* and *lu-fang* or *yin-lu* had to secure licenses from the government before commencing operation. Generally only one house of assayance and a limited number of *lu-fang* or *yin-lu* would be permitted in a locality. The *lu-fang* in North China also performed a number of banking functions. They received deposits, made loans, and remitted money. Sometimes they issued promissory notes which circulated like bank notes in the locality.

8.35 The exchange business was carried on in Ming and Ch'ing times by *ch'ien-p'u,* "money shops," and *ch'ien-cho,* "money tables." The latter term referred to small money changers in the streets who did not have a permanent establishment. In the Ch'ing period, some money shops developed into banks of considerable size. These will be discussed in the section on native banks.

Old-style and Modern-style Banks

(*1*) *The Shansi Banks*

9.1 The *p'iao-chuang* or *p'iao-hao,* literally "draft banks," were the most celebrated native banks of the old style. Since most of them were operated by businessmen from Shansi province, they were known as Shansi banks. They were strongest in the late Ch'ing period, when they developed into a national network; and it is surmised that they did more than half of the banking business in China.

9.2 It is said that the origin of the Shansi banks may have been related to the *piao-chü* or *piao-chü-tzŭ,* an agency of protection against robbery in transportation. This type of agency was well known in the Ch'ing period. In the eighteenth and nineteenth centuries establishments of this name were found in many large towns and had in their employ a great number of private soldiers (called *piao-ping*). Under contract, these offices would deliver valuables or sometimes escort persons to a destination by furnishing the necessary guard. Often this was accomplished by making a special trip, but some establishments also made periodical trips to certain places. A charge was made either at so much per package or on the basis of the number of men furnished. Each cart thus escorted, called *piao-ch'ê,* carried a small flag of the establishment which furnished the guard. It is said that such insurance offices often had a secret understanding with the bandits, thus adding to their own reliability.

9.3 Most of these establishments were found in the northern part of China, including Manchuria. They may have originated in Shansi province, but we have no evidence for this. It is apparent that both the Shansi banks and the *piao-chü* undertook the business of sending money from one place to another. However, no details about their relationship are available except that the Shansi banks periodically or occasionally made use of the *piao-chü.* An example is found in the records of a Shansi bank in 1844. In the eighth month of that year, this Shansi bank employed three *piao-chü* soldiers to make a trip to deliver 74,000 taels of silver in three carts from Peking to Soochow. The improved mail and telegraphic services toward the end of the Ch'ing dynasty undoubtedly promoted the remittance business of the Shansi banks and rendered unnecessary the actual shipping of silver by the *piao-chü*. Consequently very few such insurance offices continued in existence until the Republican era.

9.4   Although the use of a draft or *hui-p'iao* existed already in the seventeenth century, the oldest Shansi "draft bank" cannot be traced back earlier than about 1800. At about that time a merchant named Lei Lü-t'ai from P'ing-yao-hsien in Shansi is said to have opened a dye store in Tientsin, using capital put up by a Li family of the same district. For his business Lei had to obtain various dye materials from Chungking, and he found himself constantly having to send cash over the long and arduous route from Tientsin to Chungking. As a convenience for himself and other merchants he opened an office in Chungking and set up a money order service to transfer funds to and from Chungking. The venture was so successful that about 1830 he changed his dye shop, originally named *Jih-shêng-ch'ang,* into a "draft bank" named *Jih-shêng-ch'ang,* with a different character for *ch'ang.* (The change was from "long" to "prosperous.")

9.5   Many other Shansi merchants, notably those dealing with silk and cotton cloth, followed Lei's example in setting up "draft banks" and opening branch offices throughout the country for money transfer. Apparently the trade of Manchuria and Mongolia with China proper, which had long been financed by Shansi businessmen, contributed to the development of Shansi banks. In any case, it seems more than probable that their original accumulation of capital was based largely upon trade. It is also noteworthy that a number of Shansi banks continued their commercial investment as a sideline throughout the Ch'ing period. In addition to dye materials and dry goods, they also dealt with other commodities like tea, grain, and copper.

9.6   Most of the Shansi banks had their head offices in Shansi province. They were centered in the three districts of Ch'i-hsien, T'ai-ku, and P'ing-yao, and were loosely organized into three groups corresponding to the three districts. Consequently the groups were often called *Ch'i-T'ai-P'ing* or *Ch'i-T'ai-P'ing San-pang.* The oldest of the three groups was the *P'ing-yao,* which had a broader operating area and stricter rules than the other two. Otherwise there was little difference in the groups.

9.7   The Shansi banks operated branches in important cities all over the country, although their greatest strength was concentrated north of the Yangtse. At one time or another there were thirty-one "draft banks" in

Peking, twenty-five in Tientsin, twenty-three in Hankow, twenty-one in Shanghai, sixteen in Chungking, and nine in Canton. Some "draft banks" had as many as thirty branches in different places.

9.8 As indicated by their name, the main business of the "draft banks" was the transfer of funds through the issue of drafts. Sometimes, the banks were also called *hui-tui chuang,* "remitting banks." The government relied heavily on their services in transmitting revenues and expenditures. In addition to a remittance charge, profit was also made by manipulation of the different scales and grades of fineness of silver. The banks also derived income from loans and deposits. Since a considerable portion of government funds was deposited with them, the Shansi banks in a sense were fiscal agents for the national and provincial treasuries. The banks also served as agents for people who wished to purchase degrees, ranks, offices, or promotions. Occasionally the banks backed up promising candidates for offices by advancing money to them. When such a candidate became appointed as the administrator of a locality, the bank which had helped him would establish a branch in that place. To return the patronage, the administrator would authorize the branch to handle much of the business of the local treasury. In some cases, the newly-appointed official agreed to employ an agent of the bank to receive his emoluments and regulate his expenditures until the loan was repaid. This method of expanding business was also used by businessmen other than those of Shansi. But undoubtedly the relation between the Shansi banks and official circles was particularly close.

9.9 The Shansi banks were mostly family businesses. They were capitalized at amounts varying from 100,000 to 500,000 taels. The capital however made up only the *yin-ku* or "silver shares" of a bank. In addition, *shên-ku,* "personal shares," or *jên-li ku,* "man-power shares," were assigned to staff members of the bank. The "silver shares" and "personal shares" shared the profit according to percentages agreed upon in a contract. A surplus reserve was often set aside, and was known as *hu-pên,* "capital protection" for the owners, and *hu-shên,* "personal protection" for the staff. This profit-sharing system, although occasionally found in other business, was carried out most effectively in pawnshops and Shansi banks.

9.10 Another characteristic of the Shansi banks was the special precaution taken by the owners about their employees. This is best described in a report made in 1892 by Mr. T. W. Wright of the Chinese Maritime Customs: "The bankers themselves, being Shansi men, employ only natives of that province, and, when possible, select men out of their own villages. When a man is appointed to a post at one of the branch offices, his family is taken charge of by the bank and held as security for fidelity and good behavior. At his post the employee may send no letter to his family, except an open one through his master; he receives no pay or salary of any kind while away; officials are entertained, clothing is purchased as required, and sundry expenses are incurred, and every item is met with the bank's money, the strictest account being kept of all expenditures on behalf of the individual. A man holds his appointment for three years, and then returns to his employer's house, taking with him the account of the money expended during his term; he is duly searched, and the clothing he has purchased undergoes examination. Should it happen, after examination, that the accounts are satisfactory and the affairs of the bank have been prospering during the man's tenure of office, he is handsomely rewarded, and is allowed to join his family, who are immediately released. If, on the other hand, business has not prospered under the man's management and he has presented an unsatisfactory account, clothing and everything are retained, and the family are held in bondage until a suitable fine is paid, or the man himself may be imprisoned."

9.11 After 1900, Chinese revenues pledged against foreign loans or indemnities began to be deposited in foreign banks. Thus the Shansi banks lost their monopoly of government business. Other old-style native banks and the modern-style Chinese banks absorbed much of the business originally given to the Shansi banks. When the Hu-pu Bank was organized in 1905, Shansi banks were invited to join. The invitation was rejected. Movements advocated by certain Shansi people to reorganize the Shansi banks into modern banks also failed. The 1911 revolution dealt the death blow to many Shansi banks. Only a few survived during the early years of the Republic but they ceased to exert any significant influence.

(2) Other Old-style Banks

9.12 In contrast to the nationwide network of the Shansi banks were the local banks in various nineteenth-century cities. The names of the local banks varied in different parts of the country, but in general those in Peking and Tientsin were called *yin-hao*, "silver banking shops," and those in Shanghai and Hankow were called *ch'ien-chuang*, "money banking shops." Some other names were *ch'ien-p'u, ch'ien-chü, ch'ien-hao,* and *ch'ien-tien,* which may all be rendered as "money shops." The local banks were not of the same size. In some cities they were divided into those which were members of the bankers' guild and those which were not, and the names of the two kinds were different. For instance, in Canton, member banks were called *ju-hang yin-hao,* "guild-member silver shops," or *ch'ing-hsiao yin-hao,* "casting silver shops," and nonmembers were *ch'ao-mai yin-hao,* "retail silver shops."

9.13 The local banks had their own field of business, complementary to that of the Shansi banks but distinct from it. In the nineteenth century the Shansi banks were stronger in north China and the local banks were more fully developed in the south. The business with provincial and national treasuries was a monopoly of the Shansi banks, whereas services to district or circuit (*tao*) treasuries tended to be rendered by the local banks. The Shansi banks specialized in the remittance of funds by draft between branches of the same bank. The local banks generally did not have branches, and they conducted local money exchange and issued cash notes.

9.14 In making loans, many local banks acted as intermediaries between the Shansi banks and smaller merchants. The powerful *ch'ien-chuang* in Shanghai however did their business quite independent of the Shansi banks and played a predominant role in financing the export of silk and tea. Promissory notes issued by such banks were called *chuang-p'iao* in Chinese and known as "native bank orders" in English. These orders were negotiable, and those issued by firms of good standing were almost as good as cash. All the leading foreign banks accepted native bank orders through the guaranty of their compradors. Many well-established foreign business houses accepted such orders without certification and released the goods against them.

9.15 The *ch'ien-chuang* or local banks in Shanghai were divided into three classes. The largest and strongest were the *hui-hua chuang.* They were members of a clearing association, the *Hui-hua tsung-hui.* These banks had the largest capital and enjoyed the most public confidence in their *chuang-p'iao.* The next class in terms of business activity and size was the *t'iao-ta ch'ien-chuang.* The term *t'iao-ta* was interpreted by one authority as "to jump and strike," but this interpretation does not sound reasonable. A more likely interpretation is that *t'iao-ta* stands for *t'iao-tan,* "carrying load," because in the old days copper cash was carried in loads at the two ends of a pole on the shoulder of the carrier. In Shanghai, *t'iao-ta* and *t'iao-tan* are both pronounced like *t'iao-tang.* The smallest local banks were called *ling-tui ch'ien-chuang* because *ling-tui* or money exchange was their specialty. Sometimes the second and third classes were subdivided into two groups each. The four groups were called *Yüan-tzŭ-chuang, Hêng-tzŭ-chuang, Li-tzŭ-chuang,* and *Chên-tzŭ-chuang,* i.e., local banks of the grades A, B, C, and D. Together with the *hui-hua chuang,* they formed five classes.

9.16 The clearing association, or the *Hui-hua tsung-hui,* in Shanghai provided its member banks with daily facilities to square their accounts without the use of large quantities of silver. It is not clear whether the clearinghouse arrangement was a Chinese innovation. The earliest example was the *kuo-chang,* "offset accounts," system in Ningpo, which might have been used already in the eighteenth century. Since many Shanghai banks were operated by businessmen from Shaoshing and Ningpo, these Chekiang people may have introduced the system to Shanghai. In the north the *lu-fang* or silver-casting firms in Yingkow also offered clearing services for local money dealers in the nineteenth century.

9.17 In Peking before 1911 there were two types of local banks, the *yin-hao* and *ch'ien-p'u.* The former accepted deposits, made loans, issued silver and cash notes, and dealt in silver taels. The latter had smaller capital resources and dealt mainly in the exchange of silver and copper. However, the distinction between the two was not sharp, and some shops displayed a *ch'ien-p'u* signboard outside and a *yin-hao* sign inside.

9.18 A number of semiofficial banks were reported in Peking in the Hsien-fêng era (1851–1861). These banks received government funds as their capital, but their operation was generally in private hands. In 1860 five *kuan-yin-hao* or "government silver banking shops" went bankrupt. Each of the five banks had as a part of its name the character *yü.* Consequently they were known collectively as *wu-Yü,* "the five *Yü* banks." After their failure the Board of Revenue proposed in a memorial that the government honor the debt and reopen the banks, and it was ordered that an audit be made and guarantors be found for the banks. The proprietor and guarantor of the bank *Yü-shêng* were from Shansi, those of *Yü-hêng* were from Chekiang, and those of *Yü-fêng* were from Chihli (Hopei). Information about the two other banks is incomplete.

9.19 Not only was the government attempt to reopen the *Yü* banks unsuccessful, but more semiofficial money shops in Peking were in trouble the following year. Four of these were known collectively as *ssǔ-Ch'ien-hao,* "the four *Ch'ien* shops," because their names all started with the character *ch'ien.* Apparently they were founded about 1852 to issue cash notes for the Board of Revenue. Five other banks were called *wu-T'ien-hao,* "the five *T'ien* shops," because *t'ien* was the first character in their names. The five *T'ien* shops were under the sponsorship of the Office of the Imperial Household, and probably existed before 1852. They also issued cash notes. In the sixth month of 1861, due to an oversupply of cash notes issued by the four *Ch'ien* and five *T'ien* shops, the exchange rate of these government notes to silver and copper cash declined rapidly. In order to save the situation, the

Board of Revenue ordered private money shops to issue convertible cash notes of their own. This was a measure to force the money shops to circulate their copper coins in the market. Early in the following month new notes were issued by private money shops. However, the depreciation of government notes did not stop, and soon afterwards, the private notes also declined in value. Failing to appropriate funds to redeem the government notes, the authorities simply abandoned the nine semiofficial money shops.

9.20 Another famous group of semiofficial money shops in Peking were the *ssŭ-ta-Hêng* or the four big *Hêng* banks. It is reported that they may have existed as early as Ming times, but there is no evidence to substantiate this claim of seniority. At any rate, they were of great importance in the latter part of the nineteenth century, especially after the failure of the five *Yü* banks. Large amounts of public and private funds were deposited with them. Their cash notes enjoyed the confidence of the city. Three of the four banks, *Hêng-li, Hêng-hsing,* and *Hêng-yüan,* were still in business in 1908, but the fourth, *Hêng-ho,* had failed a few years earlier when a fire in the office of the Board of Revenue had precipitated a bank run.

9.21 Outside of Peking, semiofficial banks were set up in many Chinese provinces beginning in 1896. These were called *kuan-yin-hao* or *kuan-ch'ien-chü.* In addition to issuing notes, these old-style banks served as fiscal agents for local treasuries, forwarded tax funds to the government, received deposits, and made loans, often to small local banks. Toward the end of the Ch'ing dynasty, several of the *kuan-yin-hao* were reorganized into modern-style provincial banks called *shêng-yin-hang.* In the first years of the Republic, these old-style and modern-style provincial banks fell into the hands of local warlords and were utilized for reckless issuance of paper currency.

9.22 In the last decades of the nineteenth century, there was also a system of customs' banks, called *hai-kuan kuan-yin-hao.* These specialized local banks were set up in treaty ports to collect, hold in deposit, and forward the sums paid by merchants in payment of customs duties. They varied from an individual banker to organizations employing thirty, forty, or more persons. The customs bankers were designated by local Chinese authorities and operated to a large extent independent of the foreign-controlled customs service. The customs service paid the bank nothing, or at most only a small allowance for expenses, but the banks often found a good profit in handling customs funds. Some of these banks were not restricted to the customs business, but carried on all sorts of other activities, sometimes under another name. These banks declined after 1900, because, following the settlement of the Boxer troubles, the Chinese customs fund became a pledge for foreign loans, and gradually the foreign banks became the depositories of the funds necessary to meet these pledges.

(3) Modern Banks

9.23 Modern-style banks are known in Chinese by the name *yin-hang,* literally "silver guild" or "silver market." The term seems to have been used originally to refer to the guild of silversmiths or market of silver traders in T'ang and Sung times, but in modern China it is used simply as the equivalent of the English word "bank." The abridged form of *yin-hang* is *hang.* Thus, the head office of a bank is called *tsung-hang,* "the main bank," and the branch offices may be called *fên-hang,* "branch banks," or *chih-hang,* "sub-branch banks," according to their status.

9.24 All the early modern-style banks in China were branch offices of foreign banks, especially those of the British. Beginning with the Oriental Banking Corporation or *Tung-fang yin-hang,* which opened its premises in Shanghai in 1848, the British enjoyed forty years of virtual monopoly of the foreign banking business in China. This position was maintained chiefly by two influential houses, the Chartered Bank of India, Australia and China and the Hongkong and Shanghai Banking Corporation. In the 1890's, German, Japanese, Russian, and French banks pushed into the China market as part of growing international rivalry for spheres of interest. American banks entered China in 1902 and those of other western countries followed later. This period of expansion lasted well over three decades until about 1926. To reduce international competition, a number of consortia or *yin-hang-t'uan* were formed after 1913 to offer loans to the Chinese government. Member banks of the consortia, however, continued to operate quite independently.

9.25 The foreign banks operated entirely free from Chinese laws, and in China they were largely free from their own national regulations. The largest part of their credit business was the financing of foreign trade. In addition, they made profits by floating Chinese government loans and by transmitting remittances to and from China. The foreign banks enjoyed a practical monopoly of the foreign exchange business and thus dominated the exchange rates between China and the outside world until about 1930. They held on deposit large amounts of funds, private and official, notably the Chinese customs and salt revenues which had become pledges against foreign loans. In the earlier periods the foreign banks issued bank notes which circulated freely, but this practice later declined along with the improvement in the Chinese national currency.

9.26 Following is an alphabetical list of what may be termed principal foreign banks. The date indicates the year in which the bank first maintained offices in China:

Western Name	Chinese Name	Nationality	Date
American Express Co.	Mei-kuo yün-t'ung yin-hang	America	1918
American Oriental Banking Corporation	Mei-fêng yin-hang	America	1918
Asia Banking Corporation	Yu-Hua yin-hang	America	1919
Banca Italiana per ler Cina (formerly Banca Sino-Italiana)	Hua-I yin-hang	Italy	1920
Bank of China, Japan, and the Straits	Hui-t'ung yin-hang	Britain	1891
Bank of Chosen	Ch'ao-hsien yin-hang	Japan	1918
Bank of Taiwan	T'ai-wan yin-hang	Japan	c. 1913
Banque Belge pour l'Étranger	Hua-Pi yin-hang	Belgium	1902
Banque de l'Indochine	Tung-fang hui-li yin-hang	France	1899
Chartered Bank of India, Australia and China	Mai-chia-li yin-hang	Britain	1857
Chase Bank (formerly Equitable Eastern Banking Corporation)	Ta-t'ung yin-hang	America	1921
Deutsch-Asiatische Bank	Tê-Hua yin-hang	Germany	1889
Hongkong and Shanghai Banking Corporation	Hui-fêng yin-hang	Britain	1865
Mercantile Bank of India (formerly Chartered Mercantile Bank of India, London and China)	Yu-li yin-hang	Britain	1854
Mitsubishi Bank	San-ling yin-hang	Japan	1917
Mitsui Bank	San-ching yin-hang	Japan	1917
National City Bank of New York (formerly International Banking Corporation)	Hua-ch'i yin-hang	America	1902
Nederlandsche Handel-Maatschappij	Ho-lan yin-hang	Holland	1903
Oriental Banking Corporation	Tung-fang yin-hang	Britain	1848
P. and O. Banking Corporation	Ta-Ying yin-hang	Britain	1922
Russo-Chinese Bank	Tao-shêng yin-hang	Russia	1911
Sumitomo Bank	Chu-yu yin-hang	Japan	1916
Yokohama Specie Bank	Hêng-pin chêng-chin yin-hang	Japan	1892

9.27   The first modern-style Chinese bank was the *Chung-kuo t'ung-shang yin-hang,* organized in 1897. Although official backing was instrumental in its founding, the bank was essentially a private commercial organization. Its English name was originally the Imperial Bank of China, which was later changed to the Commercial Bank of China. The head office of the bank was in Shanghai. Evidently the Yangtse delta was the cradle of modern Chinese private banking. Prior to the fall of the Ch'ing dynasty, several other commercial banks had been organized in this area. The concentration of banking business in the Yangtse delta was accelerated in the Republican era. But the tendency was also balanced by a political factor. Since the main business of the modern-style Chinese banks was the financing of government, a large number of private banks maintained their headquarters in Peking while it was the national capital. The political and economic center of China became more or less identical when the Nationalist government established itself in Nanking.

9.28   The Ch'ing government's first venture in modern national banking was the Hu-pu Bank, set up in 1905, with a main office in Peking and with branches in Tientsin and Shanghai. The Hu-pu or Board of Revenue proposed the bank in a memorial of March 16, 1904, and the Peking office was opened September 27, 1905. In 1908 the institution was reorganized to become the Ta Ch'ing Bank, and since the revolution of 1911 it has been known as *Chung-kuo yin-hang* or the Bank of China. Another early government bank was *Chiao-t'ung yin-hang* or the Bank of Communications, organized in 1907. In the first decades of the Republic these two official banks competed vigorously with each other but both maintained their relatively important positions. They proved to be a stabilizing influence during several financial crises which occurred in this period.

9.29   After the Nationalist revolution, the *Chung-yang yin-hang* or Central Bank of China was established in Shanghai in 1928. A *Chung-yang yin-hang* had existed in Canton and another in Hankow during the revolution, but the one set up in 1928 was intended to become "the State Bank of the Republic of China," in other words, the real bank of banks. In the same year, the Bank of China was reorganized to become a special institution for international exchange, and the Bank of Communications was reorganized for "the purpose of fostering and developing the industries and trade of the whole country." These three banks formed a central banking group, which was joined in 1935 by the *Chung-kuo nung-min yin-hang,* or the Farmers Bank of China. The four banks were referred to collectively as *Ssŭ-hang.*

As a group, they handled the treasury's funds, issued legal-tender notes, and held control over foreign exchange and the internal money market. The division of function which was intended to develop among them did not, however, materialize to any appreciable extent.

X

Loans and Interest Rates

10.1 In the introductory chapter, it has been pointed out that a typical loan in traditional China was on short term, at a high rate of interest, and for consumer expenditure. This chapter will introduce certain details about these features, and present other major problems concerning credit. It will begin with technical terms related to loan contracts, proceed to a discussion of legal restrictions on, and government participation in, loan-making activities, and conclude with a comparison of rates of returns in the different forms of "investment" in its broader sense.

10.2 In ancient times, roughly speaking pre-Ch'in, a loan contract seems to have been made in two parts, one held by the lender and the other by the borrower. When the debt was collected, the two parts were tallied as evidence. The parts were known as *tso-ch'üan* and *yu-ch'üan*, "the left and right parts of a contract." Ancient texts, however, disagree on whether the left or the right part was held by the lender and represented his claim.

10.3 From Ch'in and Han times on, the two parts were replaced by a single contract signed by the borrower and held by the lender. The contract may have been written on a wooden or bamboo tablet, a piece of silk, and, after the second century, a piece of paper. Among the manuscripts discovered in Tun-huang and other places on the northwestern frontier of China, there are some thirty contracts datable from the eighth to the tenth century. Of the thirty contracts, ten concerned loans of cash, and the rest grain, silk, or cloth.

10.4 Here is the translation of a specimen:

On the 12th day of the 7th month in the 3rd year of Chien-chung (782), since Ma Ling-chih, a soldier, was badly in need of money and could not obtain it anywhere else, he borrowed from Ch'ien-ying, a monk of the Hu-kuo Monastery, one thousand cash. The interest for this sum will be [one] hundred cash, i.e., 10 per cent, per month. If Ch'ien-ying himself needs money, Ma Ling-chih will be obliged to repay both the principal and interest. Failing this, he will permit Ch'ien-ying to seize his property like livestock as recoupment. He will not claim the difference even if this represents a premium. For fear that faith should not be kept, this private contract has been drawn up to indicate a joint agreement of both parties. "Finger marks" have been made as evidence.

Creditor

Borrower Ma Ling-chih, age 20;
Co-borrower Tang Êrh-niang, his mother, age 50;
Co-borrower Ma Êrh-niang, his younger sister, age 12.

10.5 The word "one" before "hundred" is supplied because the text is somewhat mutilated. The "finger marks" or *hua-chih* are not to be confused with fingerprints. They were three or four dots or short lines drawn to indicate the two top sections or all three sections of one's forefinger or middle finger. They were made beside the names of the borrower, the coborrowers, and probably also that of the creditor. The standard practice was for a man to use a finger of his left hand and a woman her right. Sometimes a sketch of the whole finger was made. These finger marks were used to represent or accompany a signature and to serve as a means of identification. They were sometimes replaced by brush marks in the shape of a cross or the like. Finger marks on contracts were common in T'ang, Sung, and Yüan times. Similar practices also existed in other Far Eastern countries, including Japan, Korea, and Annam.

10.6 In this contract, the Chinese expression for borrower is *chü-ch'ien-jên* and that for coborrower is *t'ung-ch'ü-jên*. This is in accordance with the usage of T'ang times when borrowing was called *chü, pien,* or *tai,* and lending *ch'u-chü, ch'u-pien,* or *ch'u-tai.* These expressions were found in contracts and other legal documents. The word *chieh,* "to lend or to borrow," was rarely used in the T'ang period but has become the standard expression since the Sung. The T'ang expressions gradually went out of use in Sung and Yüan times.

10.7 Alongside the names of the borrower and coborrower, one may find that of a *k'ou-ch'êng-jên,* "surety promiser," *pao-jên,* "guarantor," or *chien-jên,* "witness," with their signatures or finger marks, or both. In case the principal debtor failed to repay the loan or disappeared, the coborrower, surety-promiser, guarantor, and witness would be held responsible for both the principal and the interest, or occasionally for only the principal. This responsibility was often specified in the contract.

10.8 No period of loan is indicated in this contract; probably the money was to be repaid on demand. In most of the other preserved contracts of about T'ang date, the period was from three to six months. In case the debtor failed to make the repayment at the end of the period, he would be charged additional interest according to *hsiang-yüan-li* or a "practice of the locality." This was often stated in a clause in the contract. The repayment could also be made by services rendered to the creditor. The seizure of the property of the debtor was called *ch'ien-ch'ê* or *ch'ê-tuo*. According to the T'ang legal code, one who seized more than was necessary for recoupment was subject to punishment.

10.9 In most contracts of T'ang date, the interest is specified by its amount. In the one translated above, the amount of one hundred cash is given under the phrase *mei-yüeh t'ou-fên shêng-li,* which probably means a 10 per cent interest per month. In T'ang times, interest was reckoned on a monthly basis in terms of *fên,* i.e., per cent. Since the Sung period, another word *li* has been added to mean one tenth of a *fên,* i.e., per mille. In addition, the word fên has acquired a new meaning, "one-tenth, or 10 per cent." Thus a *fên* may mean either 10 per cent or 1 per cent, and a *li* either 1 per cent or 1 per mille. Ordinarily the larger *fên* and *li* are used to refer to an annual rate, whereas the smaller *fên* and *li* refer to a monthly rate. When a 10 per cent interest rate is charged per month, the rate is called *ta-i-fên* to distinguish it from *i-fên,* 1 per cent.

10.10 Two major changes, therefore, have taken place since the Sung period with regard to the technique of charging interest. One is the use of an annual rate in addition to the monthly rate; the other is the introduction of the unit *li* as one-tenth of a *fên.* The former helps to omit the interest charged in an intercalary month; the latter provided a convenient unit for a lower rate. Both changes point to a reduction of interest in later times as compared with the T'ang period. The same tendency is also reflected in government regulations on interest from the T'ang dynasty on. The reduction, however, was by no means universal. Nor was it in great amount.

10.11 Government regulations on interest rates existed as early as the Former Han period when certain princes lost their titles because they had charged too much interest on loans to people in their principalities. History gives no information about the exact limitation. Judging from regulations of later dynasties, the Han limit may have been something like 100 per cent per annum. Such a limit, however, did not apply in emergency cases. In the year 154 B.C., when seven princes jointly revolted against the Emperor, other princes and nobles were sent out to fight the rebels. In order to equip themselves and their subordinates, these nobles supporting the Emperor had to raise a war loan. Unable to predict the outcome of the war, most money-lenders refused to respond. Only one moneylender ventured to offer a large sum, but demanded an interest of 1000 per cent per year. The investment proved to be profitable because the rebellion was suppressed in a few months. This probably was a record-breaking case of high-interest charges.

10.12 The Han historian Ssǔ-ma Ch'ien reported that the rate of return from businesses was from one-fifth to one-third of the investment per year. He, however, considered the one-third rate too greedy and added that the normal rate of returns from trading and moneylending was 20 per cent. This may have been true in the first part of the Former Han period, but was apparently not the case by the beginning of the Christian era. When Wang Mang introduced his government loans in order to help the needy people, he charged a 3 per cent interest rate per month. This must have been a reasonable rate because these loans were supposed to be philanthropic in nature. However, the rate is equivalent to 36 per cent per annum, which is higher than the rate charged by greedy businessmen in the first part of the Former Han period. If the data are reliable, we may assume that there was an increase in interest rate from the second century to the first century B.C.

10.13 Regulations on interest rates also existed under the Northern Wei dynasty. A decree in 511 prohibited the accumulation of interest to more than the amount of the original principal. This rule, known in later times as *i-pên i-li*, "one principal, one interest," was repeated from dynasty to dynasty from the T'ang period on. Generally speaking, compound interest, known as *i-li wei-pên*, "to convert interest into principal," was illegal. These rules actually would apply only when the debtor had paid neither the interest nor the principal for a long period. Ordinarily, the interest would be paid periodically and the amount of the loan would remain the same.

10.14 Beginning with the T'ang dynasty, we have figures of the highest rates of interest which were legally permitted. In the early part of the T'ang period, the ceiling rate was 6 per cent per month for private loans but 7 per cent per month for government funds. From about 728, it was 4 per cent per month for the former and 5 per cent for the latter. The Sung dynasty copied the T'ang regulations and set the rates at 4 per cent and 5 per cent per month. The Yüan, Ming, and Ch'ing dynasties lowered the ceiling rate further to 3 per cent per month. In order to study the actual application of these rules, we shall cite cases of government and private loans in the different periods.

10.15 Under the T'ang dynasty, government funds for investment were often entrusted to merchants and rich households known as *cho-ch'ien ling-shih*, "money-catching clerks," and *cho-li-ch'ien-hu*, "interest-catching households." The funds were called *kung-hsieh pên-ch'ien*, "office funds," or

shih-li pên-ch'ien, "interest-receiving funds," because the interest was used
to pay salaries to officials or to meet general expenses of government offices.
According to the estimate of a modern scholar, the total of such funds at
times in the seventh and eighth centuries may have amounted to 1,500,000
strings of cash. The interest charged by the government was about 8 per
cent per month in the first part of the seventh century. The rate was reduced to 7 per cent after about 650 and to 5 per cent after 728 in accordance
with regulations.

10.16 The ceiling rates of interest laid down by the T'ang dynasty
do not seem to have applied to loans of government grain to the people,
which was known as *kung-hsieh mai-su,* "office wheat and millet," similar to
the *kung-hsieh pên-ch'ien* or "office funds." A preserved financial account
of "office wheat and millet" from Tunhuang is probably datable to the
eighth or ninth century. It reveals that the interest charged on such government grain was 50 per cent for the period from the sixth month to the
fall, i.e., the seventh month to the ninth month. Evidently in this case the
monthly rate could not have been lower than 12.5 per cent, which is much
higher than the rate of interest charged on government funds. Remarkable
enough, loans of grain in modern China also yield more interest than loans
of money. According to statistics issued by the Central Bureau of Agricultural Experimentation in 1933, farmers paid an average of 85.2 per cent
annual interest charges on grain loans but 34 per cent on money loans.

10.17 The T'ang government, however, did not always charge its
people such exorbitant rates of interest. Public grain from the ever-normal
granary was available as loans to farmers at a reasonable rate of interest. A
financial account of 765 gives the interest on such loans as 30 per cent for
a period from the second month to the tenth month. The monthly rate was
3.75 per cent. The main function of the ever-normal granary was to stabilize
prices of grain by purchasing when there was a surplus and selling when
there was a shortage. Loans made from the granary would encourage production and consequently help to achieve stabilization because there was a
shortage more frequently than a surplus of grain.

10.18 A similar arrangement was the *Ch'ing-miao ch'ien,* "Green-
sprout money," introduced in 1069 by the Sung statesman Wang An-Shih.
Money from the funds of the ever-normal granary was lent to farmers in
the spring and collected in the autumn. The interest charged for the period
was 20 per cent for the most part of China and 30 per cent for the Ho-pei
area. Followers of Wang An-Shih in 1095 even reduced the interest rate
to 10 per cent. This well-intended measure, however, was not always car-

ried out successfully. One common abuse was that the officials in charge, fearing a failure in collecting the government money, tended to force rich farmers to take the loan whereas the needy farmers were denied the privilege. The "green-sprout money" was discontinued in the twelfth century.

10.19 Wang An-shih also introduced a *Shih-i fa* "Trading system," which operated from 1072 to 1085. Government funds or commodities were lent to people who, paying a 20 per cent interest per annum, were permitted to use the loans to do business. Strong objection was raised against the system, because the ruling classes in general were against a close association of government and trade and because professional money-lenders disliked the government competition in their field of activity. The measure was even more short-lived than the "green-sprout money."

10.20 The Yüan government and nobles entrusted funds known as *Wo-t'o ch'ien,* "ortoγ money," to Uighur businessmen and charged a monthly interest at 0.8 per cent, which was only about one-fourth of the prevailing 3 per cent rate. *Ortoγ* is from the Turkish word *ortaq* meaning "partners" or "guildmen." These privileged merchants used the funds in moneylending and various other business enterprises including foreign trade. In making loans, they sometimes charged an interest of 100 per cent per annum and converted interest into principal every year, so that in ten years, the principal and compound interest would amount to 1024 times the original principal. This was known as *yang-kao-êrh-li,* "young lamb interest."

10.21 A government office was established in 1267 to supervise the activities of the Uighur merchants. It was called *Wo-t'o tsung-kuan-fu,* "Central Bureau supervising the *ortoγ* merchants." Branch bureaus called *Wo-t'o chü* or *Wo-t'o so* were set up in places. In 1281 the name of the central office was changed to *Ch'üan-fu ssǔ,* "Supervising Money Bureau," and the funds lent to Uighur merchants became known as *Ch'üan-fu ying-yün-ch'ien.* The office and funds were abolished in 1311. *Ying-yün* was a common term referring to the practice of doing business with liquid funds. Households which were entrusted with government funds under the Liao and Chin dynasties were known as *yün-wei hu* and *ying-yün hu,* respectively. *Yün-wei* was perhaps a corrupted form of *ying-yün.* Many of these households were apparently Uighur forerunners of the *ortoγ* merchants. The term *Ch'üan-fu* alluded to the famous moneylending office described in the *Chou-li.* This semilegendary tradition also inspired the reformers Wang Mang and Wang An-shih to introduce systems of lending government funds.

10.22   Information about rates of interest on private loans from T'ang times down indicates that the legal ceiling rates were not enforced. Nevertheless, there was a tendency to charge somewhat lower rates in later periods. Interest recorded on T'ang loan contracts was mostly 6–10 per cent per month. A twelfth-century scholar, Yang Shih, stated that the normal annual interest at his time was 50–70 per cent and sometimes as high as 100 per cent. In other words, the normal monthly rate was about 4–6 per cent and the highest rate was about 8 per cent per month. A thirteenth-century work, the *Yüan-shih shih-fan,* gives valuable details on contemporary rates of returns. Pawnbroking, trading, moneylending, and similar activities generally would yield a return equal to the capital or principal in three years. In moneylending, a monthly rate of 3–5 per cent was considered reasonable. Occasionally, one might charge as high as 10 per cent per month. As for loans of grain, 30–50 per cent per term of harvest (presumably about six months) was reasonable and 80 per cent was too high. The normal rate of the Yüan period was 3 per cent per month, although the famous "young lamb interest" was over 8 per cent per month. Under the Ming dynasty, a fifteenth-century scholar-official, Yang Chi-shêng, mentioned in his will to his sons that the normal rate of interest on loans of silver was 60 per cent per year, i.e., 5 per cent per month. Taking all the above figures into consideration, we may conclude that the rate of interest on private loans dropped from 6–10 per cent per month in T'ang times to 3–5 per cent in the Sung, Yüan, and Ming periods.

10.23   Under the Ch'ing dynasty, particularly from the eighteenth century on, there was a tendency to charge even lower rates. This is shown in interest charged by pawnbrokers, in interest on government funds entrusted to businessmen, and in interest on deposits and loans related to the famous Shansi banks.

10.24   Rates of interest in pawnbroking were fixed by regulations promulgated by various local governments. In general, the ceiling rate was 3 per cent per month in the eighteenth century, and 2 per cent after the nineteenth century. The rate, however, varied with the size of the loan. For instance, the practice in Hu-chou, Chekiang province, toward the end of the seventeenth century was to charge 1.5 per cent per month if the pledged article was valued at 10 taels or more, 2 per cent if it was worth one tael and above, but 3 per cent if under one tael. A public-spirited man, T'ung Kuo-t'ai, agitated for a correction of this unfavorable rate on articles of small value. For this he was imprisoned. Later some people tried unsuccessfully to stop him with money. For thirteen years, he fought nobly against the overwhelming influence of pawnbrokers. Eventually the governor of the province ruled that a uniform 1.5 per cent rate should be adopted for all pledges. Naturally T'ung became a hero to the grateful poor.

10.25   In the year 1780, a directive from the governor of Chekiang stated that pawnshops in the provincial capital, Hangchow, charged 2 per cent per month for pledges valued under one tael, 1.5 per cent on those from one tael up, 1 per cent on those from ten taels up, and 0.8 per cent on those from fifty taels up. It was ordered that the pawnshops in other districts of the province should all adopt the same rule and have this and other rules printed from wood blocks and posted in front of each pawnshop. It is, however, doubtful whether the rules were strictly observed in all districts.

10.26   The Ch'ing dynasty frequently entrusted public funds to businessmen like pawnbrokers and salt merchants for investment. This was known as *fa-shang shêng-hsi,* "entrusted to merchants to produce profit." The interest charged by the government was on the average 2 per cent per month in the eighteenth century and 1 per cent in the nineteenth. As a rule, the interest was earmarked for a purpose, for instance, as scholarships for students in public schools, for famine relief, or for the maintenance of an orphanage. The Yung-chêng Emperor (1723–1735) ordered that special funds be granted to troops stationed in different regions, the interest from which was to be used by the soldiers for expenses in marriages and funerals. One example was in 1729 in Honan province where a fund of 4000 taels was entrusted to fifteen pawnshops at the rate of 2 per cent per month. It was assumed that the pawnbrokers would charge 3 per cent on loans, of which 1 per cent was to be their commission.

10.27   In 1882, Tso Tsung-t'ang, viceroy of Liangkiang, ordered pawnshops under his jurisdiction to reduce their interest to 2 per cent per month. In order to help the pawnbrokers, it was ruled that public funds entrusted to them should receive no more than 1 per cent interest regardless of the nature and purpose of the funds. At this time, pawnbrokers in villages and small towns complained that the 2 per cent interest rate was not adequate because frequently they received agricultural implements as pledges which were of small value but which required much handling and large storage space. This may have been one reason why pawnshops charged high interest rates on articles of small value. Apparently a part of the interest represented handling charges.

10.28   Arising in the eighteenth century and expanding in the nineteenth, the Shansi bankers held an extraordinarily cautious policy regarding interest rate. As a rule they would pay only 0.2 to 0.3 per cent per month on their deposits and charge only 0.8 to 0.9 per cent on their loans. Their good faith, however, attracted large deposits from private individuals, which, added to money from government treasuries, frequently totaled eight to twenty times their capital. As a result, interest rates in large cities were lowered substantially in the first part of the nineteenth century. For instance, letters between branches of Shansi banks reported that the interest rate in 1844 was only 0.4 to 0.5 per cent per month in Peking and 0.6 per cent in Soochow.

10.29   This 0.4, 0.5, or 0.6 per cent rate presumably was charged for short-term loans among bankers themselves. If this assumption was correct, the rate was similar to the *yin-ch'ai,* or so-called native interest, which was 0.6–0.9 per cent per month in the late nineteenth and early twentieth centuries. Modern banks and traditional banks other than those operated by Shansi bankers in this period in general paid interest of 0.4–0.8 per cent per month on fixed deposits and charged 0.7–1.2 per cent on their loans. Thus, their rates of interest were higher than those of the Shansi bankers. Actually the Shansi bankers were able to maintain lower rates largely because the money from government treasuries was deposited with them either at a very low interest payment or at none at all. This unusual practice was discontinued in the early years of the twentieth century when government banks were organized to represent the national and local treasuries.

10.30   In spite of the lower interest rates in large cities, usury remained a common feature in villages and corners of cities in the eighteenth and nineteenth centuries and as late as the early decades of the twentieth century. A famous form of usury has been known as *yin-tzŭ ch'ien,* literally, "seal-print money," which goes back at least as far as the early eighteenth century. The loans were to be repaid in monthly or daily installments, and when the payment was made the collector would stamp a seal in an account book held by the debtor as a record. Hence the term *yin-tzŭ,* "seal-stamp" or "seal-print." A common method to pay back the loan was in ten monthly installments, each of which equal to 13 per cent of the loan. On the surface, the interest rate was the legal ceiling rate of 3 per cent. Actually, since each installment included a part of the principal, if one considered the rate of interest in the first month to be 3 per cent, that in the last month would be 30 per cent. The average monthly rate was a little over 5 per cent. Another trick was to write in the contract a fictitious sum as the loan. For instance, one might write 100 taels when the real loan was only 80 taels.

The legal ceiling rate of the Republic was 2 per cent per month, but it did not affect the money sharks.

10.31 That the rate of return was different in different forms of investment was realized in ancient times. In the Former Han period, there was a proverb saying:

> "For the poor to seek riches
> Farming is not as satisfactory as crafts;
> Crafts are not as good as trading.
> To prick embroidery does not pay
> As much as leaning upon a market-door."

Moneylending was not mentioned explicitly in the proverb, but its rate of return tended to be as high as that of trading, if not higher. This seems to have been true not only in Han times but practically throughout imperial China. From the Sung period on, moneylending and trading were often mentioned together as *ying-yün,* i.e., to do business with liquid funds. It is remarkable that "investment" in land was not considered as *ying-yün.*

10.32 An interesting book entitled *Ch'ên-chou-fu i-t'ien tsung-chi* or "Comprehensive account on the communal welfare land in the prefecture Ch'ên-chou," contains valuable figures which throw light on the rates of return. In the year 1825, Lei Ch'êng-p'u, the prefect of Ch'ên-chou, Hunan, encouraged the people in the prefecture to raise a fund to purchase *i-t'ien* or communal welfare land. The grain produced from the land was to be stored in the *i-ts'ang* or communal welfare granary, to be used for the stabilization of grain price and for famine relief. Communal welfare granary was a common feature in Chinese history, and at that time there was already one in the prefecture. The unusual feature, therefore, lies in the provision of the land to produce a reliable income.

10.33 According to the account, 9475.1 strings of cash were used to purchase 250.2 *mu* of water-land. Rent from the land amounted to 505.307 *shih,* which consisted of 55 per cent of the produce. Current prices of grain in that year were 1250 and 1150 cash per *shih.* If we take the average price of 1200 cash per *shih,* the value of the 505.307 *shih* would be 606.368 strings of cash. The rate of return from this land was only 6.4 per cent per year. Even if we take the higher price, it still would not reach 7 per cent.

10.34 Out of the remaining fund, 410 strings of cash were used to purchase the grounds and buildings for two stores. In one case the price was 210 strings and in the other 200. Rent from the two stores was 22 strings each per year. The rate of return thus ran from about 10.5 per cent to 11 per cent per year, considerably higher than that from land. The rent from the stores was earmarked for the salary of the manager and assistant manager of the communal welfare granary.

10.35 Also from the fund 129.55 taels of silver were deposited to a pawnbroker. The interest was 1.5 per cent per month, not including the intercalary month. This income was used to pay the taxes and levies on the communal welfare land. A silversmith received for deposit 1600 strings of cash at the annual rate of 15 per cent and 1000 strings at the monthly rate of 1.5 per cent, not including the intercalary month. The interest from the 1600 strings was for the repair of the granary and the salary of the manager and the assistant manager of the communal welfare land. That from the 1000 strings was for the salary of government clerks in the *Liang-fang* or "Grain Section," who were assigned to assist in the management of the communal welfare land and granary. It was also for the provisions of the *tou-chi* or "bushelmen," who actually handled the grain.

10.36 From the above account, it becomes clear that deposits to a pawnbroker or a silversmith would yield an annual return from 15 per cent to 18 per cent; rent from the ground and building of a shop would be 10.5 per cent to 11 per cent; and rent from land amounted to only less than 7 per cent. Of course land rent may have been the least stable of the three returns because of the fluctuation in the price of grain. But the year 1825 seems to have been a normal year in Ch'ên-chou, which fact certainly adds to the significance of the figures in the account.

10.37 Facing this obvious difference in rates of return, the question arises why people still invested in land. The answer is that high rate of returns was not the only consideration. Small risk and high prestige were two major factors which had made investment in land attractive. A landlord was readily acceptable as a member of the ruling class if he was not one already. In addition, the owner of real estates was considered a reliable party to participate in negotiations because he could not very easily run away leaving his property behind. From the investor's point of view, it may also have been preferable in the long run to have a small but steady income which could have come only from land. An illustration may be cited from the 1814 edition of the *Shê-hsien hui-kuan lu,* or record of the club house of the townsmen from Shê-hsien, Anhwei. The club house was founded in Peking in 1563 and rebuilt in 1742. The efforts of establishing and reviving it were both supported largely by officials and tea merchants from that district. In the bylaws of the club house in 1742 and 1805, there is repeated a warning that any unused public funds of the club house should be invested only in the purchase of real property to receive rent and not to be lent for interest, in order to avoid risks. It was only about 1814 that this rigid rule was changed. From that time on unused funds were entrusted to the manager of the year to be loaned out at an interest rate of one per cent per month. Undoubtedly for safety's sake, the rate of interest expected was relatively low. Both the principal and the interest were to be passed to the next manager at the end of the year.

10.38 An eloquent advocator of "investment" in land was the seventeenth-century scholar-official Chang Ying. In a small book entitled *Hêng-ch'an so-yen* or "Miscellaneous remarks on the permanent property," Chang admits that the return from investment in land is small, and probably amounted to no more than 30 to 40 per cent of that from businesses like shopkeeping, pawnbroking, and moneylending (in other words, *ying-yün*). On the other hand, land offers several advantages in the long run. For instance, unlike many other things, land can be rejuvenated by means of fertilization and cultivation. Unlike other valuables, land can neither be destroyed nor stolen. Unlike other valuables, land cannot be readily sold. This lack of convertibility, apparently an inconvenience, actually may have helped a descendant to keep his inherited land for a longer period of time, since the possibility of converting into a large sum of ready money was difficult. Moreover, it was easier to collect rent from a farmer-tenant than from a shopkeeper tenant, because peasants are generally good-natured and merchants have the reputation of being "wicked" or tricky. Thus even among real property land is superior to buildings. Of course, one can repeat the indestructibility of land as another factor in its superiority over houses.

10.39 It must be noted that Chang Ying was speaking not only for himself but also for many investors in imperial China. As has been pointed out in the introductory chapter, the traditional ideology and other non-economic forces tended to prevent economic principles from operating to the full. Thus in a contented society with limited business activities there was a vicious circle between high rates of interest and small accumulations of liquid capital. The same situation explains why a considerable difference continued to exist between the returns from agriculture and those from other forms of investment. The limited development of money and credit reflects the nature of traditional China. In order to reform the Chinese society both economic and noneconomic changes will be necessary.

Notes

Notes

CHAPTER I

HISTORICAL SURVEY

1.1 There are two comprehensive bibliographies on Chinese money. One is A. B. Coole, *A Bibliography on Far Eastern Numismatics* (Peking, 1940), which lists works in Chinese and Japanese. The other is H. F. Bowker, *A Numismatic Bibliography of the Far East* (New York, 1943), which covers the literature in Western languages.

1.4 See the lengthy discussion by Ch'üan Han-shêng on "natural economy" in medieval China in the *Bulletin of the Institute of History and Philology* (Academia Sinica) 10(1942).75–176. An article by Ho Tzǔ-ch'üan in the *Liu-t'ung pieh-lu*, Li-chuang, 1945, pp. 1–36, has pointed out the continuation of coinage in south China.

1.8 On the Two-tax system or Liang-shui fa, see Chü Ch'ing-yüan, *T'ang-tai ts'ai-chêng shih*, Ch'ang-sha, 1940, pp. 28–55. On the Single-whip system or *I-t'iao-pien fa*, see articles by Liang Fang-chung in *Studies in Modern Economic History of China* (Academia Sinica) 4.1(1936).1–65, and *Chinese Social and Economic History Review* (Academia Sinica) 7.1(1944).115–119.

1.10 For references of the second century B.C., see *Shih-chi* (Wu-chou t'ung-wên ed., same for the other dynastic histories) 129.16a, *Han shu* 4.20a, 91.6a.

1.11 *Han shu* 47.4b, 99C.29b.

1.12 *Ch'a-ch'ao Ho Shên chia-ch'an ch'ing-tan* in the *Chung-kuo nei-luan wai-huo li-shih ts'ung-shu*, Shanghai, 1946, pp. 277–280 and Okutaira Masahiro, *Tōa senshi*, Tōkyō, 1938, 13.26a–27a. Also see the *Ch'ing shih-lu*, Chia-ch'ing, 37.49b–50a.

1.15 For the term *tzǔ-ch'ien chia*, see *Han shu* 91.11a. The cases of nobles practising usury are recorded in *Han shu* 15A.23a, 15B.30b.

1.18 For the early history of pawnshops, see Lien-sheng Yang, "Buddhist Monasteries and Four Money-raising Institutions in Chinese History," *Harvard Journal of Asiatic Studies* 13(1950).174–178.

1.19 See Lien-sheng Yang, *op. cit.*, 179–182.

1.26 Dr. Hu Shih in an essay published in 1926 states that the characteristic of Oriental civilization is its contentment and that of Western civilization is its discontent. See *Hu Shih wên-ts'un*, 3rd Series, Shanghai, 1930, pp. 6–18. Similar observation has been made by Ku Ch'un-fan in his *Chiu wên-ming yü hsin kung-yeh*, Shanghai, 1945, pp. 36–55.

CHAPTER II

MANIFOLD AND MISCELLANEOUS CURRENCY

2.2 *I-ching* (*Shih-san-ching chu-su* ed.) 8.2b.

2.4 Wang Ming-yüan, *Hsien-Ch'in huo-pi shih*, Canton, 1947, pp. 27–45.

2.5 *Kuan-tzŭ* (*Ssŭ-pu ts'ung-k'an* ed.) 22.6b; *Han shu* 24B.3a. For class distinction in the use of money, see Max Weber, *General Economic History,* translated by F. H. Knight, Glencoe, 1927, p. 238.

2.6 After writing this chapter, I had opportunity to read proofs of Wang Yü-ch'üan's interesting book, *Early Chinese Coinage* in August, 1951. Certain differences in interpretation have been incorporated in the notes to this chapter.

2.7 Kuo Mo-jo, *Shih-p'i-p'an shu,* Chungking, 1945, p. 10; Wang Ming-yüan, *op. cit.,* pp. 14–27; Wang Yü-ch'üan, *op. cit.,* p. 64.

2.9 *Shih-chi* 30.18b, translated by R. C. Blue, "The Argumentation of the Shih-huo chih," *Harvard Journal of Asiatic Studies* 11(1948).12.

2.11 H. E. Gibson, "The Use of Cowries as Money during the Shang and Chou Period," *Journal of the North China Branch of the Royal Asiatic Society* 71(1940).40–42.

    Wang Yü-ch'üan, however, labels the reconstruction of Gibson as "unrealistic," and suggests that "the 'double string' is a single string curved at the middle with its pendent ends equal in length and with each end bearing an equal number of cowries" (*op. cit.,* p. 84).

2.12 Finds of ant-nose money have also been made in the provinces of Anhwei and Kiangsu. It has been pointed out that this particular form of money may have been a currency in the state of Ch'u in the period of Warring States. Wang Yü-ch'üan, *op. cit.,* pp. 76–83.

2.13 *Han shu* 24B.20a–21b; Nancy Lee Swann, *Food and Money in Ancient China,* Princeton, 1950, pp. 325–334.

2.14 Ichimura Sanjirō, *Shinashi kenkyū,* Tōkyō, 1939, pp. 27–50. Ichimura distinguishes a coastal "cowry culture" to the south of China and an inland "jade culture" to the east.

2.15 Excellent illustrations of spade and knife coins may be found in two important works on numismatics, namely, Ting Fu-pao, *Ku-ch'ien ta-tz'ŭ-tien,* Shanghai, 1938, and Okutaira Mashahiro, *Tōa senshi,* Tōkyō, 1938. A survey on spade and knife coins by Katō Shigeru is in *Tōhō gakuhō,* Tōkyō, 5(1934). Recently, Wang Yü-ch'üan has made an extensive study in his *Early Chinese Coinage,* New York, 1951.

2.17 Wang Yü-ch'üan dates the "hollow handle" spade c. 400 B.C., but considers certain prototypes of spade coins as early as the beginning of the Chou period (*op. cit.,* p. 129). This early date of coinage, as well as his date of the Ch'i knives (see below), seems doubtful.

2.19 Wang Yü-ch'üan suggests that the knife coins which bear the inscription *Ch'i-tsao-pang ch'ang-fa-huo* may have been circulated in the first half of the ninth century B.C. when Duke Hsien of Ch'i first established his capital in the modern Shantung province (*op. cit.,* pp. 152–153).

2.20 For *Wang-tao,* see *Mo-tzŭ* (*Ssŭ-pu ts'ung-k'an* ed.) 10.15a. For *fa-ch'ien,* see *Han shu* 24B.4b, Swann, *op. cit.,* pp. 235–236.

2.21 Lien-sheng Yang, "Notes on Dr. Swann's *Food and Money in Ancient China,*" *Harvard Journal of Asiatic Studies* 13(1950).556.

2.22 *Han shu* 24B.20a–21b, 25a–b; Swann, *op. cit.,* pp. 325–334; Lien-sheng Yang, "Notes on the Economic History of the Chin Dynasty," *Harvard Journal of Asiatic Studies* 9(1946).117, 175–185.

2.23 *Chin shu* 26.18b–19a; *Wei shu* 110.15b–16a; *Sui shu* 24.20b–21a. Also see note 1.4.

2.24 Katō Shigeru, *Tōsō jidai ni okeru kingin no kenkyū,* Tōkyō, 1924, pp. 14–86.

2.25 *Ts'ê-fu yüan-kuei,* 501.4a, 15a–b.

2.26 Yüan Chên, *Yüan-shih Ch'ang-ch'ing chi* (*Ssŭ-pu ts'ung-k'an* ed.) 34.5a, Arthur Waley, *The Life and Times of Po Chü-i*, New York, 1949, p. 139. Hsü Hung-tsu in his travels reported the use of salt as money in Kweichow in the seventeenth century. See *Hsü Hsia-k'o yu-chi*, edited by V. K. Ting, 1928, 8.2,7; "Salt Cakes as Current Coins" (in Yunnan), *American Journal of Numismatics* 13.3(1879).56.

2.27 See article by Ch'üan Han-shêng in the *Bulletin of the Institute of History and Philology* 20(1948).202.

2.28 For discussions on the 100 and 200 cash tablets, see Ting Fu-pao, *op. cit., hsia-pien*, 465b–468a.

2.30 *Yüan-tien-chang* (Shên's ed.) 20.30b; Yao Sui, *Mu-an chi* (*Ssŭ-pu ts'ung-k'an* ed.) 14.8a.

2.31 An excellent collection is in the Museum of the American Numismatic Society.

CHAPTER III

ROUND COINS FROM ANTIQUITY TO THE END OF THE CH'ING DYNASTY

3.1 *Han shu* 24B.1a–b; Swann, *Food and Money in Ancient China*, pp. 221–222.

3.2 *Shih-chi* 129.2b; Swann, *op. cit.*, p. 422.

3.3 *Han shu* 24B.2b–3a; Swann, *op. cit.*, pp. 225–227; Ting Fu-pao, *Ku-ch'ien ta-tz'ü-tien, hsia-pien*, 471a–478b; Ting Fu-pao, "Ku-ch'üan-hsüeh kang-yao," in *Ku-ch'ien*, Kuei-lin, 1942, p. 1.

3.4 Ting, *Ku-ch'ien ta-tz'ü-tien, tsung-lun*, 36a–37a; Okutaira, *Tōa senshi*, 6.22a–28b; Wang Yü-ch'üan, *Ancient Chinese Coinage*, pp. 187–205.

3.5–3.9 *Han shu* 24B.3a–b, 10a–b, 14a–b, 19a; Swann, *op. cit.*, pp. 229–233, 268, 271, 291–294, 323–324, 377–382; Lien-sheng Yang, "Notes on Dr. Swann's *Food and Money in Ancient China*," *Harvard Journal of Asiatic Studies* 13(1950).556.

3.10–3.14 *Han shu* 24B.19a–21a, 25a–b; Swann, *op. cit.*, pp. 324–332, 348–352, 383; Yang, *op. cit.*, 556–557.

3.15 Bernhard Karlgren, *The Book of Odes*, Stockholm, 1950, p. 244; Wang Yü-ch'üan, *op. cit.*, pp. 90–114.

3.17 Ting, *Ku-ch'ien ta-tz'ü-tien, hsia-pien*, 379b, 385b–387a; Okutaira, *op. cit.*, 9.24a–27a.

3.19 Ting, *op. cit.*, 384a–385a.

3.22 Ting, *op. cit., tsung-lun*, 55a–b.

3.24 See article by Wang Ching-ju in *Bulletin of the Institute of History and Philology* 3.2(1931).277–278.

3.25 Okutaira, *op. cit.*, 14.18a–20a; Nishimura Shinji, *Nihon kodai keizai, kōkanhen*, Tōkyō, 1933, 4.133–135.

3.26–3.28 Chang Chi-yen, *Chung-kuo chin-yung lun*, Shanghai, 1930, pp. 44–47; "Dollar-copper exchange in China," in *The Chinese Economic Bulletin* 8(1926). 363–364.

3.29 Katō Shigeru, *Tōsō jidai kingin no kenkyū*, pp. 418–419; Okutaira, *op. cit.*, 13.94a–95b.

3.30 *Chin shu* 26.16b–19a; Lien-sheng Yang, "Notes on the Economic History of the Chin Dynasty," *Harvard Journal of Asiatic Studies* 9(1946). 175–185.

3.31 *Sui shu* 24.20b–21b.

3.32 Miyasaki Ichisada, *Godai sōsho no tsūka mondai*, Kyōto, 1943, pp. 93–96.

3.33 Miyasaki, *op. cit.*, pp. 118–121, 165–169.

3.34 Chu Hsieh, *Chung-kuo huo-pi wên-t'i*, Chungking, 1940, pp. 35–39.

3.35 When the Chin dynasty occupied the Shansi area, they abolished the iron cash there and permitted its exportation to the Mongols, who melted the coins to make military weapons. This was an important factor in the rise of the Mongols. Wang Kuo-wei, *Hei-Ta shih-lüeh chien-chêng* (*Hai-ning Wang Ching-an hsien-shêng i-shu* ed.) 18b–19a.

CHAPTER IV

SOME GENERAL PROBLEMS CONCERNING ROUND COINS

4.1 *Han shu* 24B.3b–6a; Swann, *Food and Money in Ancient China*, pp. 232–240. For a comprehensive discussion of private coinage, see Hozumi Fumio, *Shina kaheikō*, Kyōto, 1944, pp. 83–130.

4.2 *Wei shu* 110.15a; *Sung shu* 75.14a–b; *Wên-hsien t'ung-k'ao* (*Shih-t'ung* ed.) 8.89a–b, 9.93a–b.

4.3 *Wei shu* 110.19a; *Wên-hsien t'ung-k'ao* 8.89a–90b.

4.4 *Sui shu* 24.23a–b; *An Lu-shan shih-chi* (*Hsüeh-hai lei-pien* ed.) A.13a.

4.5–4.6 *Han shu* 24B.3b–4b; Swann, *op. cit.*, pp. 232–238; Hozumi, *op. cit.*, pp. 108–117.

4.7 *Sui shu* 24.22a; *Sung shih* 180.22b.

4.8 *Sung shih* 180.13a–14a; *Ch'ing-ch'ao hsü wên-hsien t'ung-k'ao* (*Shih-t'ung* ed.) 19.7691b–7692a.

4.9 Hozumi, *op. cit.*, pp. 90–91; *Ch'ing-ch'ao wên-hsien t'ung-k'ao* (*Shih-t'ung* ed.) 199.6636a.

4.10 See article by Katō Shigeru in *Shigaku* 12.2(1933).

4.12 *Han shu* 24B.1b–3a; Swann, *op. cit.*, pp. 222–228.

4.13 *Chin shih* 48.18a; *Yüan shih* 93.20b–21a.

4.14 *Han shu* 24B.14a–b; Swann, *op. cit.*, pp. 291–294; *Sung shih* 180.1a, 13a–18a.

4.18 H. B. Morse, "Currency and Measures in China," *Journal of the China Branch of the Royal Asiatic Society* 24.1(1889).58–75.

4.19 Liu Yüeh-yün, *Kuang-hsü k'uai-chi piao* (1901 ed.) 1.6a–8a, 2.1a–b.

4.20 Okutaira, *Tōa senshi* 8.11a–14b.

4.21 *I-lin* (*Ssu-pu ts'ung-k'an* ed.) 1.53a.

4.22–4.23 *Sui shu* 24.21a–b; Ting Fu-pao, *Ku-ch'ien ta-tz'ŭ-tien, tsung-lun*, 5b–6a; Hozumi, *op. cit.*, pp. 181–185.

4.24–4.25 Chang Hung-chao, *Shih-ya*, Peking, 1927, pp. 337–346.

4.26–4.27 Ting Fu-pao, *op. cit.*, 7a–b mentions six occasions in Chinese history when Buddhist statues were destroyed to obtain copper for coinage.

On copper control and "copper famine," see article by Araki Toshikazu in *Tōyōshi kenkyū* 4.1(1948).1–29.

A term analogous to *ch'ien-huang* is *yin-huang*, "silver famine." It has been used to refer to the acute shortage of silver in the second quarter of the nineteenth century. See article by T'ang Hsiang-lung in *Shê-hui k'o-hsüeh tsa-chih* 1.3(1930).1–31 and article by T'ai-p'ing shan-jên in *Chung-ho yüeh-k'an* 1.8 (1940) .61–75.

4.28 *Sung shih* 180.21a–21b.

4.29 John Hall, "Notes on the Early Ch'ing Copper Trade with Japan," *Harvard Journal of Asiatic Studies* 12(1949).441–461.

4.30 T'ang Yü-k'un, *Chih-ch'ien t'ung-k'ao* (1852 ed.) 2.8a–26b, 2.32b–33b, 3.3b–28a. On silver shortage in this period, see articles mentioned in note 4.26–4.27.

CHAPTER V

GOLD AND SILVER

5.1 The most important work on the history of gold and silver in China is Katō Shigeru, *Tōsō jidai kingin no kenkyū*, Tōkyō, 1924. Although the book deals primarily with the T'ang and Sung periods, it also contains much information on earlier and later times.

5.3 Kuo Mo-jo, *Liang-Chou chin-wên-tz'ŭ ta-hsi, k'ao-shih*, Tōkyō, 1925, 12a–13b.

5.4 *Shu-ching* (*Shih-san-ching chu-su* ed.) 19.11b–12a; James Legge, *The Chinese Classics*, 3.605–606.

5.5 Wang Yü-ch'üan, "The Distribution of Coin Types in Ancient China," *American Numismatic Society, Museum Notes* 3(1948).147–148.

5.6 *Han shu* 24B.3a; Swann, *Food and Money in Ancient China*, pp. 228–229; Katō, *op. cit.*, pp. 365–369.

5.7 Katō, *op. cit.*, pp. 369–375.

5.8 Chang Nai Chi, *An Inscribed Chinese Ingot of the 12th Century A.D.* (Numismatic Notes and Monographs no. 103), New York, 1944, pp. 1–3.

5.9 *Han shu* 24B.20a; Swann, *op. cit.*, p. 327.

5.10 Katō, *op. cit.*, pp. 684–688.

5.11 I am indebted to Mr. Wang Yü-ch'üan for the information. A silver piece bearing a similar inscription of the same date is reported in Okutaira, *Tōa senshi* 8.10a–b. Instead of *Shang-chün t'ing-chang*, Okutaira reads *Shang-chün t'ing-hou*, *t'ing-hou* being a noble rank of Han times.

5.12 Throughout the period under discussion, silver was used as a medium of exchange in the modern provinces of Kansu and Kwangtung, which border Chinese Turkestan and French Indo-China, respectively.

5.13 Okutaira, *op. cit.*, 9.34a–36b.

5.14 Chang Nai Chi, *op. cit.*, pp. 4–9; Okutaira, *op. cit.*, 10.89b–91a.

5.15–5.16 Katō, *op. cit.*, pp. 725–729.

5.17 Katō, *op. cit.*, pp. 496–538.

5.18 Katō, *op. cit.*, pp. 539–573.

5.19 *Chin shih* 48.8a–10a.

5.20 On foreign trade and silver movement, see Robert P. Blake, "The Circulation of Silver in the Moslem East down to the Mongol Epoch," *Harvard Journal of Asiatic Studies* 2(1937).291–328; Kotake Fumio, *Kinsei shina keizaishi kenkyū*, Tōkyō, 1942, pp. 39–43; article by Momose Hiroshi in *Seikyū gakusō* 19(1935).90–147; and article by Liang Fang-chung in *Chinese Social and Economic History Review* 6.2(1939).267–324.

On *chin-hua yin* in the Ming period, see article by Horii Kazuo in *Tōyōshi kenkyū* 5.2(1939).40–52.

5.21 Katō, *op. cit.*, pp. 290–291. My interpretation of the term *chung-chin* is based on *Shih-chi* 30.7b, where the text reads, "The yellow metal (i.e. gold) is the superior kind, the white metal (i.e. silver) is the intermediate, and the red metal (i.e. copper) is the inferior."

5.22 P. O. Sigler, *Sycee Silver* (Numismatic Notes and Monographs no. 99), New York, 1943, pp. 1–28. On the term *sa-hua*, see P. Pelliot, *T'oung pao* 32(1936).230–237.

5.23 H. B. Morse, *The Trade and Administration of China*, London, 1920, pp. 169–183; Hirohata Shigeru, *Shina kaheishi sensōkō*, Tōkyō, 1933, pp. 123–162.

5.24 *Shina keizai sensho* 5.622–624, Hirohata Shigeru, *op. cit.*, pp. 164–176, Chang Chi-yen, *Chung-kuo chin-yung lun*, pp. 232–235.

5.25 Katō, *op. cit.*, pp. 475–476, 721–724; Miyasaki Ichisada, *Godai sōsho no tsūka mondai*, p. 238; H. B. Morse, *The Chronicles of the East India Company Trading in China, 1635–1834*, Oxford, 1926, 2.7, 41; Le P. Pierre Hoang, *Notions techniques sur la propriété en Chine*, Shanghai, 1897, p. 43 and Ch'ü Hsüan-ying, *Chung-kuo shê-hui shih-liao ts'ung-ch'ao*, Shanghai, 1937, pp. 330–332.

5.26 A. P. Andrew, "The End of the Mexican Dollar," *Quarterly Journal of Economics* 18(1904).321–356; Hozumi Fumio, *Shina kahei kō*, pp. 43–49.

5.27–5.28 Ch'ü Hsüan-ying, *op. cit.*, pp. 343–344; Liang Ssŭ-tsê, *Yin-ching fa-mi*, 1844 ed., 1.28a–32a, 2.38a–42a; S. W. Williams, *The Chinese Commercial Guide*, Hongkong, 1863, p. 268.

5.29 Chang Chi-yen, *op. cit.*, pp. 28–35.

5.30–5.32 For specimens see C. C. Tsiang, *Illustrations of Chinese Gold, Silver and Nickel Coins*, Shanghai, 1939.

5.33 *Ch'ing shih kao*, 130.3b.

CHAPTER VI

PAPER MONEY TO THE END OF THE SUNG DYNASTY

6.2 *Han shu* 24B.10a–b; Swann, *Food and Money in Ancient China*, pp. 268–269.

6.3–6.5 T'ao Hsi-shêng and Chü Ch'ing-yüan, *T'ang-tai ching-chi shih*, Shanghai, 1936, pp. 108–110. Also see article by Hino Kaisaburō in *Shien* 22, 23, 25 (1938–41). One reason for the prohibition of *fei-ch'ien* or *pien-huan* by the T'ang government was to prevent the hoarding of copper coins among the people and to increase the circulation of actual cash in the market.

6.6–6.9 On the origin and development of paper money in the Northern Sung period, see articles by Katō Shigeru in *Shigaku* 9.3(1931), 15.1(1938) and *Shigaku zasshi* 45.1(1934) and articles by Hino Kaisaburō in *Shigaku zasshi* 45.2, 3(1934) and *Shakaikeizaishigaku* 8.1, 2, 3(1948).

On *chieh* or period of circulation of *chiao-tzŭ*, see Chu Hsieh, *Chung-kuo huo-pi wên-t'i*, pp. 75–80.

6.10–6.11 On paper notes in the Southern Sung period, see articles by Sogabe Shizuo in *Shakaikeizaishigaku* 7.7, 8(1937), by Hino Kaisaburō in *Shigaku zasshi* 48.7, 8, 9(1937) and *Shakaikeizaishigaku* 12.9(1941), and by Katō Shigeru in *Tōyō gakuhō* 28.4(1941).

6.12 The Ming work is the *Shu-chung kuang-chi* by Ts'ao Hsüeh-ch'üan (*Ssŭ-k'u ch'üan-shu chên-pên ch'u-chi* ed.) 67.13a–23b. It quotes Fei Chu of the Yüan period.

6.13 On the meanings of the terms *chiao-tzŭ, hui-tzŭ*, and *kuan-tzŭ*, see article by Katō Shigeru in *Tōhō gakuhō*, Tōkyō, 6(1936).

6.15 See article by Katō Shigeru on the circulation of silver in the Southern Sung period and the relation between silver and *hui-tzŭ* in *Tōyō gakuhō* 29.3, 4(1944). 603–610.

6.16 Okutaira, *Tōa senshi*, 10.92a–93a.

6.17–6.22 *Sung shih* 181.4a–11b.

6.23–6.26 *Tōyō rekishi daijiten* 3.78. See article by Hino Kaisaburō, *Tōyō gakuhō* 23.1(1935).

6.27–6.38 *Chin shih* 48.5a–23b. Five Chin notes, of which two are fragmentary, are reproduced and discussed in Lo Chên-yü, *Ssŭ-ch'ao ch'ao-pi t'u-lu* (1914 ed.). 1a–5b. A note of 1214 is discussed by Jos. Mullie in *T'oung pao* 33(1937).150–157.

Paper Money: Part II

CHAPTER VII

PAPER MONEY FROM THE YÜAN DYNASTY
TO THE END OF THE CH'ING DYNASTY

7.1 On paper currency of the Yüan period, see article by Ch'üan Han-shêng in *Shih-liao yü shih-hsüeh* 1(1944).1–57, article by Wu Han in *Chinese Social and Economic History Review* 7.2(1946).79–106, and Herbert Franke, *Geld und Wirtschaft in China unter der Mongolen-Herrschaft*, Leipzig, 1949, pp. 34–106.

7.2 *Yüan shih* 150.11b–12a; Ch'üan Han-shêng, *op. cit.,* p. 9.

7.3 Wu Han, *op. cit.,* pp. 79–80.

7.4 *Yüan shih* 146.6b; W. W. Rockhill, *The Journey of William of Rubruck to the Eastern Parts of the World*, London, 1900, p. 201.

7.5–7.7 *Yüan shih* 4.2b, 93.20b. For the emendation, see Wu Han, *op. cit.,* pp. 103–106.

7.8–7.9 *Yüan shih* 93.21a; Ch'üan Han-shêng, *op. cit.,* pp. 11–17; Herbert Franke, *op. cit.,* pp. 40–43.

7.10–7.11 Ch'üan Han-shêng, *op. cit.,* pp. 20–30.

7.12 For illustrations of bronze blocks for the printing of Yüan notes, see Okutaira, *Tōa senshi* 11.73a and article by L. C. Goodrich in the *American Numismatic Society Museum Notes* 4(1950).127–130.

7.13–7.16 Wu Han, *op. cit.,* pp. 93–98.

7.17 Max Weber, *Gesammelte Aufsätze zur Religionssoziologie*, Tuebingen, 1920, 2.276; Robert Eisler, *Das Geld und Seine Geschichtliche Bedeutung*, Munich, 1924, p. 217.

On units of Yüan currency, see article by P. Pelliot in *T'oung pao* 27(1931).190 and article by Maeda Naonori in *Shakaikeizaishigaku* 14.4(1944).1–22.

7.18–7.20 *Yüan tien-chang* 20.11a–31b; Hozumi Fumio, *Shina kahei kō*, pp. 130–158.

For a picturesque description of corrupted practices in the administration of paper currency in the Yüan period, see verses by Liu Shih-chung in *Yang-ch'un pai-hsüeh* B3.

A bronze seal for cancellation of old and illegible notes in the Yüan period has been discovered in Kirin. See article by Inaba Iwakichi in *Seikyū gakusō* 3(1931).68–78.

7.21 Ch'üan Han-shêng, *op. cit.,* pp. 35, 41.

7.23 Chu Hsieh, *Chung-kuo huo-pi wên-ti*, pp. 52–57.

7.24 *Ming shih* 81.1b–2a. For illustration of Ming notes, see Okutaira, *op. cit.,* 12.50a, Lo Chên-yü, *Ssŭ-ch'ao ch'ao-pi t'u-lu*, pp. 7a–8a.

7.25–7.26 *Ming shih* 2b–5a.

7.27 Chi Liu-ch'i, *Ming-chi pei-lüeh* 19.15b–16a. Translation is based on that in *The North China Herald*, 1889, 43.208.

7.28 *Ch'ing-ch'ao wên-hsien t'ung-k'ao* 13.497b–c.

7.29 H. B. Morse, "Currency in China," *Journal of the North China Branch of the Royal Asiatic Society* 38(1907).29–31; Lo Chên-yü, *op. cit.,* 8b–9a; T'ang Hsiang-lung, article on the currency of the Hsien-fêng era, in *Studies in Modern Economic History of China* 2.1(1933).22–23. According to T'ang, notes representing 1000, 10000, 50000, and 100000 cash were issued in 1855.

7.30 *Tso Wên-hsiang kung ch'üan-chi, tsou-kao* 20.35a–36b; *Li Wên-chung kung ch'üan-chi, p'êng-liao han-kao* 1.49a; T'ang Hsiang-lung, *op. cit.,* pp. 19–20, 25–26.

7.31 *Jih-chih lu* (*Ssŭ-pu pei-yao* ed.) 11.39a–b.

7.32 T. R. Jernigan, *China's Business Methods and Policy*, p. 98.

7.33 Chang Chi-yen, *Chung-kuo chin-yung lun*, p. 232.

7.34 *Tōyō rekishi daijiten* 1.434b.

7.35 *Ma Yin-ch'u yen-chiang chi*, 3rd Series, Shanghai, 1929, p. 45.

7.36 Chu Hsieh, *Chung-kuo huo-pi wên-t'i*, pp. 337–357.

CHAPTER VIII

TRADITIONAL CREDIT INSTITUTIONS

8.1–8.3 Lien-sheng Yang, "Buddhist Monasteries and Four Money-raising Institutions in Chinese History," *Harvard Journal of Asiatic Studies* 13(1950).174–179.

8.4–8.5 *Chinese Economic Journal and Bulletin* 18(1936).76–80.

8.6–8.8 Yang Chao-yü, *Chung-kuo tien-tang-yeh*, Shanghai, 1932, pp. 3–7; Lien-sheng · Yang, *op. cit.* 191; *History of Banking in All Leading Nations*, New York, 1896, 4.547–567 (section on China by T. R. Jernigan).

8.9 The expression *fêng ch'ao-ch'ing* for this privilege goes back to Ch'in and Han times. The official titles *ch'ao-fêng ta-fu* and *ch'ao-fêng lang* of the Sung period seem to have led to the use of the honorary name *ch'ao-fêng* for a pawnbroker who might have held such a title.

8.10 *Chinese Economic Bulletin* 10(1927).47–48.

8.11–8.12 See article on pawnbroking in the Ch'ing period by Abe Takeo in *Haneda hakushi shōju kinen tōyōshi ronsō*, Tōkyō, 1950, pp. 15–31.

8.13 On the importance of pawning of rice to poor peasants, see Ku Yen-wu, *T'ien-hsia chün-kuo li-ping shu* (*Ssŭ-pu ts'ung-k'an* ed.) 32.31a; *Yung-chêng chu-p'i yü-chih*, Li Wei, 3.43b; Hsi Yü-fu, *Huang-ch'ao chêng-tien lei-tsuan* 1903 ed., 151.12a–15a.

8.15 Two Chinese works devoted to *ho-hui* are Wang Tsung-p'ei, *Chung-kuo chih ho-hui*, Shanghai, 1931, and Yang Hsi-mêng, *Chung-kuo ho-hui chih yen-chiu*, Shanghai, 1935.

8.16–8.17 Lien-sheng Yang, *op. cit.*, 179–182. Also see articles by Naba Toshisada in *Shirin* 23.2, 3, 4(1938) and 24.3, 4(1939).

8.18 *Hsin T'ang shu* 197.16a.

8.19–8.20 Chu Hsi, *Hui-an hsien-shêng Chu Wên-kung wên-chi* (*Ssŭ-pu ts'ung-k'an* ed.) 99.15a–22b; Wang Tsung-p'ei, *op. cit.*, pp. 4–5.

8.22–8.23 A. H. Smith, *Village Life in China*, New York, 1899, pp. 152–160.

8.24 Wang Tsung-p'ei, *op. cit.*, pp. 16, 60, 124–129.

8.25 Wang Tsung-p'ei, *op. cit.*, p. 4. The play about P'ang Chü-shih is in *Yüan-ch'ü hsüan, i-chi*, vol. 10.

8.26 Wang Tsung-p'ei, *op. cit.*, pp. 75–93.

8.27–8.32 Katō Shigeru, *Tōsō jidai kingin no kenkyū*, pp. 574–613, and his article on *kuei-fang* in *Tōyō gakuhō* 12.4(1928).

8.33 Katō Shigeru's article on the development of *ch'ien-p'u* and *ch'ien-chuang* in the Ch'ing period in *Tōyō gakuhō* 31.3(1947).

8.34 Chang Chi-yen, *Chung-kuo chin-yung lun*, pp. 232–235.

8.35 *Yung-chêng chu-p'i yü-chih*, T'ien Wên-ching, 4.104b–105b; P'u Sung-ling, *Hsing-shih yin-yüan chuan*, 1.5a.

CHAPTER IX

OLD–STYLE AND MODERN–STYLE BANKS

9.1 Two important books on the Shansi banks are Ch'ên Ch'i-t'ien, *Shan-hsi p'iao-chuang k'ao-lüeh*, Shanghai, 1937, and Wei Chü-hsien, *Shan-hsi p'iao-hao shih*, Chungking, 1944.

9.2 *Decennial Reports* 1882–1891 (China Imperial Maritime Customs Statistical Series no. 6), Shanghai, 1893, p. 19; articles by Katō Shigeru in *Shakaikeizaishigaku* 4.6 (1934), and Imahori Seini in *Tōyō bunka kenkyū* 3(2946).51–57.

9.3 Wei Chü-hsien, *op. cit.,* p. 7.

9.4 Ch'ên Ch'i-t'ien, *op. cit.,* pp. 22–31.

9.5 Ch'ên, *op. cit.,* pp. 110–114; Wei, *op. cit.,* pp. 257–258.

9.6 *Ch'i-t'ai-p'ing* means "Pray for an age of peace and prosperity."

9.7 Ch'ên, *op. cit.,* 98–108. Ch'ên cites *Shina keizai sensho* 3.567–579. *Shina keizai sensho* 6, however, gives the figures as 22 in Shanghai (pp. 568–570), 32 in Hankow (pp. 608–609), 25 in Peking (pp. 626–627), and 34 in Tientsin (pp. 618–619).

9.8 Ch'ên, *op. cit.,* pp. 152–156. *Decennial Reports* 1882–1891, pp. 518–519, 572.

9.9 Ch'ên, *op. cit.,* pp. 84–89; Yang Chao-yü, *Chung-kuo tien-tang yeh,* pp. 41–44.

9.10 *Decennial Reports* 1882–1891, p. 519; T. R. Jernigan, *China's Business Methods and Policy,* 1904, pp. 92–103.

9.11 Ch'ên, *op. cit.,* pp. 38–63.

9.12 Kuo Hsiao-hsien, article on native banks in Shanghai, *Shang-hai-shih t'ung-chih-kuan ch'i-k'an* 3(1933).803–857.

9.13–9.15 Ch'ên, *op. cit.,* pp. 156–158; George H. Chang, "A Brief Survey of Chinese Native Banks," and "The Practices of Shanghai Native Banks," in *The Central Bank of China Bulletin* 4.1(1838).25–32, 4.4(1938).310–319, 5.2(1939).134–142.

9.16 In some western works *hui-hua* is romanized as *wei-wah* in accordance with Shanghai pronunciation. For a description of *kuo-chang* in English, see *Haikwan Banking System* (China Imperial Maritime Customs Office Series no. 12), Shanghai, 1879, p. 114. A similar credit system used by Shansi banks in Mongolian trade is described in *Chinese Economic Bulletin* 8(1926).13–14.

9.17 *Shina keizai sensho* 6.628.

9.18–9.20 Wêng T'ung-ho, *Wêng Wên-kung kung jih-chi,* 1861.50a–61a., 107a; Li Tz'ŭ-ming, *Yüeh-man-t'ang jih-chi pu,* hsin-chi A.81a–b, 91a; *Ch'ing-ch'ao hsü wên-hsien t'ung-k'ao* 20.7707a; *Shina keizai sensho* 5.631.

9.21 Chang Chi-yen, *Chung-kuo chin-yung lun,* pp. 92–103.

9.22 For a survey of the Haikwan banks, see *Haikwan Banking System,* mentioned above.

9.23 By "modern-style banks" I mean those which are organized in the pattern of modern banks in the Western world.

On the original meaning of the term *yin-hang,* see article by Katō Shigeru in *Shigaku zasshi* 43.3(1932).

9.24–9.26 Kuo Hsiao-hsien, article on foreign banks in Shanghai, *Shang-hai-shih t'ung-chih-kuan ch'i-k'an* 2.2(1934).547–602. According to this article (p. 558), the puzzling name *Mai-chia-li* for the Chartered Bank of India, Australia and China may have been a transliteration of the name of John Mackellar, its first (?) president.

9.27–9.28 Kuo Hsiao-hsien, article on Chinese modern banks in Shanghai, *Shang-hai-shih t'ung-chih-kuan ch'i-k'an* 2.1(1933).441–498.

9.29 F. M. Tamagna, *Banking and Finance in China,* New York, 1942, pp. 121–149.

CHAPTER X

LOANS AND INTEREST RATES

10.2 Niida Noboru, *Tōsō horitsu bunsho no kenkyū,* Tōkyō, 1937, pp. 7–9.

10.3 Niida, *op. cit.,* pp. 226–228.

10.4 Niida, *op. cit.*, p. 253. The translation is based on that by Lionel Giles, *Six Centuries at Tun-huang*, London, 1944, p. 35.

10.5 Niida, *op. cit.*, pp. 37–60.

10.6–10.9 Niida, *op. cit.*, pp. 286–294.

10.11 *Han shu* 15A.23a, 15B.30b. Swann, *Food and Money in Ancient China*, pp. 393–398.

10.12 Swann, *op. cit.*, p. 392.

10.13 *Wei shu.* 114.18a–b.

10.14 Niida, *op. cit.*, pp. 275–277. Also see article on cancellation of public and private debts in Chinese history by Katō Shigeru in *Shirin* 10.4(1925).16–18.

10.15 Chü Ch'ing-yüan, *T'ang-tai ts'ai-chêng shih*, Ch'ang-sha, 1940, pp. 126–132.

10.16 Niida, *op. cit.*, pp. 271–273.

10.17 Niida, *op. cit.*, pp. 319–323.

10.18 For a recent study on *ch'ing-miao fa* and *ch'ang-p'ing ts'ang*, see article by Imahori Seini in *Shigaku zasshi* 56.10, 11(1946).

10.19 See article on productive loans in modern China by Miyasaki Ichisada in *Tōyōshi kenkyū* 11.1(1950).5–7.

10.20 Yao Sui, *Mu-an chi*, 13.9a. Also see article on *Wo-t'o ch'ien* by Muramachi Seini in *Tōyō gakuhō* 13.1(1942).

10.21 Lien-sheng Yang, review of Wittfogel and Fêng, *History of Chinese Society, Liao*, in *Harvard Journal of Asiatic Studies* 13(1950).222–225.

10.22 Niida, *op. cit.*, pp. 266–267; Miyazaki, *op. cit.*, p. 8. Yang's will is in *Yang Chung-min kung i-pi* (*Ts'ung-shu chi-ch'êng* ed.) p. 6.

10.24 *Hu-chou fu-chih*, 1874 ed., 77.37b. 95.24a–b.

10.25 *Ch'êng-kuei shih-i*, Supplement, 17a–b.

10.26 See article on pawnbroking by Abe Takeo, in *Haneda hakushi shōju kinen tōyōshi ronsō*, pp. 15–31.

10.27 *Tso Wên-hsiang kung ch'üan-chi, tsou-kao*, 59.65a–66a.

10.28 Wei Chü-hsien, *Shan-hsi p'iao-hao-shih*, pp. 244–245, 247–248.

10.29 *Shina keizai sensho* 5.571–572, 586–590.

10.30 Miyasaki, *op. cit.*, p. 7.

10.31 Translation by Swann, *op. cit.*, p. 434.

10.32–10.36 *Ch'ên-chou-fu i-t'ien tsung-chi*, A.19a–24b.

10.37 *Shê-hsien hui-kuan lu* 1814 ed., *hou-chi*, 15a, 18b, *hsin-chi*, 14b, 17a, 18b.

10.38 *Hêng-ch'an so-yen* (*Ts'ung-shu chi-ch'êng* ed.) pp. 2–9.

Index to Chinese Characters

Index to Chinese Characters

(The numbers refer to chapters and paragraphs. The letter n *stands for note.)*

Abe Takeo 安部健夫 8.11n

an 按 8.4

An Lu-shan 安祿山 4.4

An Lu-shan shih-chi 安祿山事蹟 4.4n

an-tien 按店 8.4

Araki Toshikazu 荒木敏一 4.26n

ch'a-ch'ao 茶鈔 6.26

Ch'a-ch'ao Ho Shên chia-ch'an ch'ing-tan 查抄和珅家產清單
1.12n

ch'a-chiao-ch'ao 茶交鈔 6.26

ch'a-chiao-yin 茶交引 6.26

Chang Chi-yen 張輯顏 3.28n

Chang Hung-chao 章鴻釗 4.24n

Chang Ying 張英 10.38

chang-ch'ien 長錢 4.21

ch'ang-ch'ien 長錢 4.21, 4.22

chang-ch'ien shan-chia 長錢善價 4.21

Chang-chou chün-hsiang 漳州軍餉 5.31

ch'ang-shêng k'u 長生庫 8.2

ch'ang-shou hui 長壽會 8.26

Chang-tsung 章宗 6.29

chan-jên yang 站人洋 5.27

ch'ao 鈔 6.23, 7.17

ch'ao-fêng 朝奉 8.9

ch'ao-fêng lang 朝奉郎 8.9n

ch'ao-fêng ta-fu 朝奉大夫 8.9n

Ch'ao-hsien yin-hang 朝鮮銀行 9.26

ch'ao-kuan 鈔貫 7.26

ch'ao-mai yin-hao 炒賣銀號 9.12

ch'ao-mu 鈔母 4.13

ch'ao-pên 鈔本 4.13

ch'ao-pi 鈔幣 6.3

ch'ao-yin 鈔引 6.23, 8.31

ch'a-yin 茶引 6.26

chê-êrh 折二 4.14

Ch'ên Ch'i-t'ien 陳其田 9.1n

Ch'ên-chou-fu i-t'ien tsung-chi 辰州府義田總記 10.32

Ch'êng-an pao-huo 承安寶貨 5.19, 6.31, 6.32

Ch'êng-kuei shih-i 成規拾遺 10.25n

ch'êng-t'i 稱提 7.23

Chên-tzǔ-chuang 貞字莊 9.15

Ch'ên-yüan 陳爰 5.5

Chên-yu pao-ch'üan 貞祐寶券 6.36, 6.37

Chên-yu t'ung-pao 貞祐通寶 6.37

chê-san 折三 4.14

ch'ê-tuo 掣奪 10.8

Chi Liu-ch'i 計六奇 7.27n

Chai I 賈誼 4.1

chiao-ch'ao 交鈔 6.23, 6.27, 6.29, 6.30, 6.33, 6.36, 7.4, 7.5

chiao-ch'ao k'u 交鈔庫 7.21

Chiao-t'ung yin-hang 交通銀行 9.28

chiao-tzǔ 交子 6.6, 6.7, 6.9, 6.11–6.13, 6.16, 6.23, 6.24, 6.27, 7.19, 8.29, 8.32

chiao-tzǔ hu 交子戶 6.6

chiao-tzǔ p'u 交子鋪 6.6, 8.29

Chiao-tzǔ wu 交子務 6.7, 6.9, 7.21

chiao-yin 交引 6.23

chiao-yin p'u 交引鋪 8.31

chieh 借 10.6

chieh 界 6.7, 6.12, 6.14

chieh-jên ch'ang-ch'ien, huan-jên tuan-pai 借人長錢還人短陌 4.21

chieh-t'ieh-tzŭ 街帖子 7.34

chieh-tien k'u 解典庫 8.3

ch'ien 錢 3.14, 3.15, 3.19, 5.7

ch'ien-ch'ao 錢鈔 6.24

ch'ien-ch'ê 牽掣 10.8

ch'ien-ch'ien 鉛錢 3.32, 4.1

ch'ien-ch'ien-wu-wu-shih 錢千無五十 4.20

ch'ien-ch'ing 錢輕 4.12

ch'ien-cho 錢桌 8.35

ch'ien-chü 錢局 4.1, 4.8, 9.12

ch'ien-chuang 錢莊 9.12, 9.14, 9.15

Chien-chung 建中 10.4

ch'ien-chung 錢重 4.12

ch'ien-hao 錢號 9.12

Chien-ho êrh-nien Shang-chün t'ing-chang chêng-chu kung-hsing 建和
二年上郡亭長正鑄公行 5.11

ch'ien-hsi ch'ien 鉛錫錢 4.7

ch'ien-huang 錢荒 4.27

chien-jêh 見人 10.7

Ch'ien-lung pao-tsang 乾隆寶藏 3.29

ch'ien-p'iao 錢票 7.29, 7.31

ch'ien-p'u 錢舖 8.35, 9.12, 9.17

chien-shou tao 尖首刀 2.19

ch'ien-ssŭ-ts'ang 千斯倉 6.16

ch'ien-tien 錢店 9.12

chien-tso 剪鑿 4.6

chien-ts'o 剪錯 4.6

chien-tsu pu 尖足布 2.17

ch'ien-yang 錢樣 4.3

ch'ien-yin 錢引 6.9-6.12, 6.24

Ch'ien-ying 虔英 10.4

Ch'ien-yin wu 錢引務 6.9

Ch'ien-yüan chung-pao 乾元重寶 4.14

Ch'i-fa-huo 齊法化(貨) 2.18

chi-fu p'u 寄附鋪 8.3

chih 質 8.4

ch'ih 勅 6.12

Chih-chêng 至正 7.15, 7.16

chih-ch'ien 制錢 4.16

Chih-ch'ien t'ung-k'ao 制錢通考 4.30n

ch'ih-chin 赤金 5.21

chih-hang 支行 9.23

chih-k'u 質庫 8.3

Ch'i-hsien 祁縣 9.6

Ch'i-hsien hui 七賢會 8.22, 8.25

Chih-ta yin-ch'ao 至大銀鈔 7.13

ch'ih-ts'ê 赤仄 4.14

Chih-yüan 至元 7.16

Chih-yüan ch'ao 至元鈔 7.12

Chih-yüan t'ung-hsing pao-ch'ao 至元通行寶鈔 7.12

Chih-yüan t'ung-pao 至元通寶 3.23

Chi-mo fa-huo 即墨法化 (貨) 2.18

chin 斤 5.4

chin 金 2.4, 5.1, 5.2, 5.6

Ch'ing shih-kao 清史稿 5.33n

Ch'ing shih-lu 清實錄 1.12n

Ch'ing-ch'ao hsü wên-hsien t'ung-k'ao 清朝續文獻通考 4.8n

ch'ing-ch'ien 輕錢 4.5, 4.10, 4.12

ch'ing-ch'ien 青錢 4.25

ch'ing-hsiao yin-hao 傾銷銀號 9.12

ch'ing-hsiao yin-p'u 傾銷銀鋪 8.33

ching-li 經理 8.9

Ch'ing-miao ch'ien 青苗錢 10.18

chin-hua yin 金花銀 5.20

chin-pai-lieh 金百爷 5.3

chin-p'u 金鋪 8.30, 8.33

chin-ssŭ 金肆 8.30

Chin-t'ang-hsien 金堂縣 5.14

chin-tao 金刀 3.11

chin-tien 金店 8.33

chin-ts'o-tao 金錯刀 3.10

Chin-tsou yüan 進奏院 6.4

chin-yin ch'a-yen chiao-yin p'u 金銀茶鹽交引鋪 8.31

chin-yin chiao-yin p'u 金銀交引鋪 8.31

chin-yin ch'ien 金銀錢 3.29

chin-yin hang 金銀行 8.30

chin-yin hsien-ch'ien kuan-tzŭ 金銀見錢關子 6.22

chin-yin p'u 金銀鋪 8.27

Ch'i-T'ai-P'ing 祁太平 9.6

Ch'i-T'ai-P'ing San-pang 祁太平三幫 9.6

Ch'i-tao 齊刀 2.18

ch'i-tao 契刀 2.21, 3.10

Ch'i-tsao-pang ch'ang-fa-huo 齊造邦長法化 2.18

Chiu wên-ming yü hsin kung-yeh 舊文明與新工業 1.26n

chiu-fu 九府 3.1, 3.2

chiu-fu yüan-fa 九府圜法 3.1

chiu-kuei 偢櫃 8.28

chiu-liu ch'ien 九六錢 4.18

chiu-pa ch'ien 九八錢 4.18

chiu-p'ai 酒牌 2.29

Chiu-pa kuei-yüan 九八規元 5.23

cho-ch'ien ling-shih 捉錢令史 10.15

cho-li-ch'ien hu 捉利錢戶 10.15

ch'ou 籌 2.28

Chou, King Ching of 周景王 4.10

chou-kuo 周郭 4.6

Chou-li 周禮 3.1, 3.2, 10.21

Chou-t'ung yüan-pao 周通元寶 3.20

Chou-yüan t'ung-pao 周元通寶 3.20

chu 貯 2.8

chü 舉 10.6

Chu Hsi 朱熹 8.19

Chu Hsieh 朱偰 3.34n

Chü Ch'ing-yüan 鞠清遠 1.8n

Ch'ü Hsüan-ying 瞿宣穎 5.25n

Ch'u, King Chuang of 楚莊王 4.10

Ch'ü, Prince Huan of 邍伯還 2.7

ch'uan 串 4.15, 4.19

ch'üan 泉 3.11, 3.14

ch'üan ch'ing-chung 權輕重 4.12

Ch'üan Han-shêng 全漢昇 1.4n

Ch'üan-fu 泉府 10.21

Ch'üan-fu ssŭ 泉府司 10.21

Ch'üan-fu ying-yün-ch'ien 泉府營運錢 10.21

chuang 莊 2.14

chuang (adult) 壯 2.14

chuang-ch'üan ssŭ-shih 壯泉四十 3.11

chuang-p'iao 莊票 9.14, 9.15

chuan-li 轉利 8.8

ch'üan-ma 犬馬 2.4

chuan-shu 篆書 3.22

Ch'uan-yin 川引 6.10, 6.18

chü-ch'ien-jên 舉錢人 10.6

chu-ch'ien-yüan 鑄錢院 4.8

ch'u-chü 出舉 10.6

Chüeh-huo wu 榷貨務 6.24

chui-hsiung chu-chi 追凶逐吉 8.16

Chu-lin ch'i-hsien 竹林七賢 8.25

chun-wu-pai-wên-shêng 準伍百文省 2.28

Ch'ung-an 崇安 8.19

chung-ch'ien 重錢 4.5, 4.10, 4.12

chung-chin 中金 5.21

chung-ch'üan san-shih 中泉三十 3.11

Chung-ho yüeh-k'an 中和月刊 4.26n

Chung-kuo chih ho-hui 中國之合會 8.15n

Chung-kuo chin-yung lun 中國金融論 3.28n

Chung-kuo ho-hui chih yen-chiu 中國合會之研究 8.15n

Chung-kuo huo-pi wên-t'i 中國貨幣問題 3.34n

Chung-kuo nei-luan wai-huo li-shih ts'ung-shu 中國內亂外禍歷史叢書 1.12n

Chung-kuo nung-min yin-hang 中國農民銀行 9.29

Chung-kuo shê-hui shih-liao ts'ung-ch'ao 中國社會史料叢鈔 5.25n

Chung-kuo tien-tang-yeh 中國典當業 8.8n

Chung-kuo t'ung-shang yin-hang 中國通商銀行 7.35, 9.27

Chung-kuo yin-hang 中國銀行 9.28

chung-pao 重寶 4.14

chung-pi 中幣 2.5

Chung-tu 中都 6.33

Chung-t'ung 中統 7.16

Chung-t'ung ch'ao 中統鈔 7.7, 7.15

Chung-t'ung chiao-ch'ao 中統交鈔 7.15

Chung-t'ung yin-huo 中統銀貨 7.6

Chung-t'ung yüan-pao-ch'ao 中統元寶鈔 7.7

Chung-t'ung yüan-pao chiao-ch'ao 中統元寶交鈔 7.7

Chung-yang yin-hang 中央銀行 9.29

Chung-yüan êrh-nien 中元二年 5.10

chu-p'ai 竹牌 2.29

ch'u-pai 除陌 4.23

ch'u-pien 出便 10.6

chü-ssŭ 局私 4.8

ch'u-tai 出貸 10.6

ch'u-tien 除墊 4.23

chu-yü 珠玉 2.4

Chu-yu yin-hang 住友銀行 9.26

êrh 二 4.14

êrh-kuan li 二貫例 6.28

êrh-kuei 二櫃 8.9

fa-ch'ien 法錢 2.20

fa-huo 法化(貨) 2.20

fang-chu 放鑄 4.1

fang-tsu pu 方足布 2.17

fan-ping 番餅 5.27

fan-yin 番銀 5.27

fa-pi 法幣 7.35

fa-shang shêng-hsi 發商生息 10.26

Fei Chu 費著 6.12n

fei-ch'ien 飛錢 6.3

fei-liang kai-yüan 廢兩改元 1.10

fên 分 10.9, 10.10

fên-hang 分行 9.23

Fu-pan 福板 5.33

Godai sōsho no tsūka mondai 五代宋初の通貨問題 3.32n

Haikwan (Hai-kuan) 海關 5.23

hai-kuan kuan-yin-hao 海關官銀號 9.22

Hai-ning Wang Ching-an hsien-shêng i-shu 海寧王靜安先生
遺書 3.35n

hai-pa 海肥(貝八) 2.14

Hai-tung t'ung-pao 海東通寶 3.25

Haneda hakushi shōju kinen tōyōshi ronsō 羽田博士頌壽紀念
東洋史論叢 8.11n

hang-chuang 行莊 5.33

Hang-pan 杭板 5.33

Hang-p'ing hua-pao 行平化寶 5.23

Han-t'ung yüan-pao 漢通元寶 3.20

Han-yüan t'ung-pao 漢元通寶 3.20

hao-ch'ien 好錢 4.5

Hei-Ta shih-lüeh chien-chêng 黑韃事略箋證 3.35n

Hêng-ch'an so-yen 恒產瑣言 10.38

Hêng-ho 恒和 9.20

Hêng-hsing 恒興 9.20

Hêng-li 恒利 9.20

Hêng-pin chêng-chin yin-hang 橫濱正金銀行 9.26

Hêng-tzŭ-chuang 亨字莊 9.15

Hêng-yüan 恒源 9.20

Hino Kaisaburō 日野開三郎 6.3n

Hirohata Shigeru 廣畑茂 5.23n

Ho Shên 和珅 1.12

Ho Tzŭ-ch'üan 何茲全 1.4n

ho-hui 合會 8.15

Ho-lan yin-hang 和蘭銀行 9.26

Horii Kazuo 堀井一雄 5.20n

hou-chi 後集 10.37n

Ho-t'ung k'ai-chên 和同開珎 3.25

Ho-t'ung k'ai-pao 和同開珎 3.25

Hozumi Fumio 穗積文雄 4.1n

Hsi Yü-fu 席裕福 8.13n

hsia-chia 下架 8.8

hsia-pien 下編 2.28n

hsiang-p'iao 餉票 7.30

hsiang-yin 餉銀 5.31

hsiang-yüan-li 鄉原例 10.8

hsiao-ch'ao 小鈔 6.28

hsiao-ch'ien 小錢 4.10, 4.16

hsiao-ch'üan chih-i 小泉直一 3.11

hsiao-p'ing-ch'ien 小平錢 4.14

hsiao-shu-ch'ien 小數錢 4.19

hsiao-yang 小洋 5.35

hsia-pi 下幣 2.5

hsi-ch'ien 西錢 4.22

hsien-ch'ien ch'ao 見錢鈔 6.24

hsien-ch'ien chiao-ch'ao 見錢交鈔 6.24

hsien-ch'ien chiao-yin 見錢交引 6.25

hsien-ch'ien kuan-tzŭ 見錢關子 6.21

Hsien-Ch'in huo-pi shih 先秦貨幣史 2.4n

Hsin-an ku-shih 新安古式 8.21

hsin-chi 新集 10.37n

hsin-chi 辛集 9.18n

Hsin-chou 信州 4.28

hsing 星 5.7

Hsing-shih yin-yüan chuan 醒世姻緣傳 8.35n

hsing-shu 行書 3.22

Hsing-ting pao-ch'üan 興定寶泉 6.37, 6.38

hsing-yung-ch'ao 行用鈔 7.3

hsi-ssŭ (sycee) 細絲 5.22

hsi-ssŭ wên-yin 細絲紋銀 5.22

Hsi-tz'ŭ 繫辭 2.2

Hsü Hsia-k'o yu-chi 徐霞客遊記 2.26n

Hsü Hung-tsu 徐宏祖 2.26n

Hsüeh-hai lei-pien 學海類編 4.4n

hsüeh-hua-yin 雪花銀 5.22

Hu Shih wên-ts'un 胡適文存 1.26n

hua-chih 晝指 10.5

Hua-ch'i yin-hang 花旗銀行 9.26

Huai-an-chün 淮安軍 5.14

Huai-chiao 淮交 6.11, 6.19

Hua-I yin-hang 華義銀行 9.26

Huang-ch'ao chêng-tien lei-tsuan 皇朝政典類纂 8.13n

huang-ch'ien 黃錢 4.25

huang-chin 黃金 5.1

huan-tu 環讀 3.17

Hua-Pi yin-hang 華比銀行 9.26

hua-yin 花銀 5.22

Hu-chou 湖州 10.24

Hu-chou fu-chih 湖州府志 10.24n

Hu-hui 湖會 6.19

Hui-an hsien-shêng Chu Wên-kung wên-chi 晦菴先生朱文公文集 8.19n

Hui-fêng yin-hang 匯豐銀行 9.26

hui-hua-chuang 匯劃莊 9.15

Hui-hua tsung-hui 匯劃總會 9.15, 9.16

hui-p'iao 會票 6.17, 7.31, 9.4

hui-p'iao (modern term) 匯票 6.17

hui-tui chuang 匯兌莊 9.8

Hui-t'ung yin-hang 惠通銀行 9.26

hui-tzŭ 會子 6.12–6.20, 6.22, 7.2, 7.5, 7.8, 8.32

Hu-Kuang hui-tzŭ 湖廣會子 6.19

Hu-kuo Monastery 護國寺 10.4

hun-ch'ao 昏鈔 7.18

Hung-wu 洪武 7.24

hun-lan 昏爛 7.19

huo 貨 2.4

huo-ch'üan 貨泉 2.22, 3.12

huo-pi 貨幣 2.4

huo-pu 貨布 2.22, 3.12

hu-pên 護本 9.9

Hu-pu pao-ch'üan-chü 戶部寶泉局 4.29

Hu-pu yin-hang 戶部銀行 7.35, 9.11, 9.28

hu-shên 護身 9.9

i 鎰 5.6, 5.7

I 益 3.3

i-chi 乙集 8.25n

i-ch'ien ch'êng-t'i 以錢稱提 7.23

Ichimura Sanjirō 市村瓚次郎 2.14n

I-ching 易經 2.2n

I-chou 益州 6.6

I Chou shu 逸周書 4.10

i-fa ch'êng-t'i 以法稱提 7.23

i-fên 一分 10.9

I-lin 易林 4.21

i-li wei-pên 以利為本 10.13

Imahori Seini 今堀誠二 9.2n

Inaba Iwakichi 稻葉岩吉 7.18n

i-pai li 一百例 6.28

i-pên i-li 一本一利 10.13

i-pi-ch'ien 蟻鼻錢 2.12

I-t'iao-pien fa 一條鞭法 1.8n

i-t'ien 義田 10.32

i-ts'ang 義倉 8.21, 10.32

jên-li ku 人力股 9.9

Jih-chih lu 日知錄 7.31n

Jih-shêng-ch'ang (draft bank) 日昇昌 9.4

Jih-shêng-ch'ang (dye shop) 日昇長 9.4

ju-chung liang-ts'ao chiao-yin 入中糧草交引 6.25

ju-hang yin-hao 入行銀號 9.12

Jun-chou 潤州 5.13

k'ai-shu 楷書 3.22

K'ai-t'ung yüan-pao 開通元寶 3.16, 3.17, 3.20-3.22, 4.14

K'ai-yüan 開元 3.17

K'ai-yüan t'ung-pao 開元通寶 3.16, 3.17, 3.19, 3.20-3.22

Katō Shigeru 加藤繁 2.15n, 2.24, 5.15, 5.21

Kinsei shina keizaishi kenkyū 近世支那經濟史研究 5.20n

kōkanhen 交換篇 3.25n

Kotake Fumio 小竹文夫 5.20n

k'o-tzŭ 錁子 5.22

k'ou-ch'êng-jên 口承人 10.7

kou-ch'ien 鉤錢 5.28

ku 穀 2.4

Ku Ch'un-fan 谷春帆 1.26n

Ku Yen-wu 顧炎武 8.13n

kuan 貫 4.15, 4.23

kuan-ch'ien-chü 官錢局 7.35, 9.21

kuan-chu 官鑄 4.1

Kuang-hsü k'uai-chi piao 光緒會計表 4.19n

kuang-pan 光板 5.27

Kuang-pan 廣板 5.33

kuan-hui 官會 6.13

kuan-li 貫例 6.28

kuan-pai 貫陌 7.19

kuan-p'iao 官票 7.29

kuan-shih 管事 8.9

Kuan-tzŭ 管子 2.5n, 3.2

kuan-tzŭ 關子 6.20, 6.21

kuan-yin-hao 官銀號 7.35, 9.18, 9.21

K'uan-yung t'ung-pao 寬永通寶 3.25

kua-tzŭ chin 瓜子金 5.22

Ku-ch'ien 古錢 3.3n

Ku-ch'ien ta-tz'ŭ-tien 古錢大辭典 2.15n

Ku-ch'üan-hsüeh kang-yao 古泉學綱要 3.3n

kuei 簋 2.7

kuei-fang 櫃房 6.6, 8.27–8.29

kuei-lien ch'ien 鬼臉錢 2.12

kuei-pei 龜貝 2.4

kung 工 5.28

kung-chü 公據 6.20, 6.21

kung-hsieh mai-su 公廨麥粟 10.16

kung-hsieh pên-ch'ien 公廨本錢 10.15, 10.16

kung-ku chü 公估局 5.24, 8.34

kung-mo ch'ien 工墨錢 7.19

Kung-pu pao-yüan-chü 工部寶源局 4.29

k'ung-shou pu 空首布 2.17

Kung-sun Shu 公孫述 3.30

Kuo Hsiao-hsien 郭孝先 9.12n

Kuo Mo-jo 郭沫若 2.7n

kuo-chang 過帳 9.16

Kuo-yü 國語 4.10

K'u-p'ing 庫平 5.23

ku-san-pai-lieh 古三百孚 5.3

Ku-shih 固始 2.12

lai 賚 2.8

lan-fan 爛番 5.27

lan-pan 爛板 5.27

lao-ch'ao 老鈔 7.20

lao-jên hui 老人會 8.26

lao-kung yin 老公銀 5.31

Lei Ch'êng-p'u 雷成樸 10.32

Lei Lü-t'ai 雷履泰 9.4

li 例 6.28

li 釐 7.13, 10.9, 10.10

Li 李 9.4

Li Tz'ŭ-ming 李慈銘 9.18n

Li Wei 李衛 8.13n

Li Wên-chung kung ch'üan-chi 李文忠公全集 7.30n

liang 兩 3.19, 4.14, 5.4, 5.6

Liang Fang-chung 梁方仲 1.8n

Liang, Imperial Prince Hsiao 梁孝王 1.11

Liang Ssŭ-tsê 梁思澤 5.27n

Liang-Chou chin-wên-tz'ŭ ta-hsi k'ao-shih 兩周金文辭大系考釋 5.3n

Liang-fang 糧房 10.35

Liangkiang 兩江 10.27

Liang-shui fa 兩稅法 1.8n

li-ch'ao 釐鈔 7.9

lieh 乎 5.3, 5.4

Lin-an-fu hsing-yung 臨安府行用 2.28

ling-tui ch'ien-chuang 零兌錢莊 9.15

li-shu 隸書 3.22

Li-tzŭ-chuang 利字莊 9.15

liu 流 5.9

Liu 劉 3.11

Liu Shih-chung 劉時中 7.18n

Liu Yüeh-yün 劉嶽雲 4.19n

Liu-t'ung pieh-lu 六同別錄 1.4n

Lo Chên-yü 羅振玉 6.27n

lu 鑪 4.4

lu-fang (loofang) 爐房 5.24, 7.33, 8.33, 8.34, 9.16

Lü-hsing 呂刑 5.4

Lung-yang 龍洋 5.32

lun-hui 輪會 8.24

Ma Êrh-niang 馬二娘 10.4

Ma Ling-chih 馬令痣 10.4

Ma Yin-ch'u yen-chiang chi 馬寅初演講集 7.35n

Maeda Naonori 前田直典 7.17n

mai (to purchase) 買 2.8

mai (to sell) 賣 2.8

Mia-chia-li yin-hang 麥加利銀行 9.26

ma-t'i chin 馬蹄金 5.21

ma-t'i yin 馬蹄銀 5.22

Mei-fêng yin-hang 美豐銀行 9.26

Mei-kuo yün-t'ung yin-hang 美國運通銀行 9.26

mei-yüeh t'ou-fên shêng-li 每月頭分生利 10.9

miao 苗 2.14

min 緡 4.15

Ming-chi pei-lüeh 明季北略 7.27n

Ming-tao 明刀 2.16, 2.18, 2.19

Miyasaki Ichisada 宮崎市定 3.32n

Momose Hiroshi 百瀨弘 5.20n

Mo-tzŭ 墨子 2.20

mu 母 4.13

Mu-an chi 牧菴集 2.30n

mu-p'ai 木牌 2.29

Muramachi Seini 村上正二 10.20n

Naba Toshisada 那波利貞 8.16n

Nan-ching 南京 6.33

Nihon kodai keizai 日本古代經濟 3.25n

Niida Noboru 仁井田陞 10.2n

Nishimura Shinji 西村真次 3.25n

o-ch'ien 惡錢 4.5

Okutaira Masaniro 奧平昌洪 1.14n, 2.15n

pai-chin 白金 5.1, 5.8

pai-lu-p'i-pi 白鹿皮幣 6.2

pai-p'ao hui 白袍會 8.26

p'ai-tzŭ 牌子 2.28

pai-yin 白銀 5.22

Pan Ku 班固 3.1

P'ang Chü-shih 龐居士 8.25

P'ang Kung 龐公 8.25

P'ang Yün 龐蘊 8.25

pan-liang 半兩 3.5-3.9, 3.16

pao 寶 2.8

pao-ch'ao 寶鈔 7.29

Pao-ch'ao t'i-chü-ssŭ 寶鈔提舉司 7.24

Pao-ch'üan 寶泉 3.24, 4.29

pao-huo 寶化 (貨) 3.3

pao-jên 保人 10.7

pao-liu-huo 寶六貨 3.3

pao-ssŭ-huo 寶四貨 3.3

pao-tsang 寶藏 3.29

Pao-yüan 寶源 3.24, 4.29

pa-tzŭ 肥 (貶) 子 2.14

pei 貝 2.8

p'êng 朋 2.7, 2.10

p'êng-liao han-kao 朋僚函稿 7.30n

pên-yang 本洋 5.27

pi 幣 2.4

piao-ch'ê 標車 9.2

piao-chü 標局 9.2, 9.3

p'iao-chuang 票莊 9.1

piao-chü-tzŭ 標局子 9.2

p'iao-hao 票號 9.1

piao-hui 標會 8.24

piao-ping 標兵 9.2

pien 便 10.6

pien-ch'ien 便錢 6.5, 6.23

Pien-ch'ien wu 便錢務 6.5

pien-huan 便換 6.3, 6.5

ping 餅 5.22

P'ing-chun hsing-yung k'u 平準行用庫 7.21

P'ing-liang-fu 平涼府 6.33

p'ing-ti liang-ts'ao chiao-yin 平糴糧草交引 6.25

P'ing-yao-hsien 平遙縣 9.4, 9.6

p'i-pi 皮幣 2.4

Po-chou 博州 7.2

pu 布 2.15, 3.11, 3.15

p'u 鏄 3.15

P'u Sung-ling 蒲松齡 8.35n

Pu-chêng-shih ssŭ 布政使司 7.30

pu-po 布帛 2.4

sa-hua yin-tzŭ 撒花銀子 5.22

San-ching yin-hang 三井銀行 9.26

san-fên ch'ien 三分錢 3.6

San-ho-t'ung chiao-ch'ao 三合同交鈔 6.33

san-kuan 三官 3.8

San-ling yin-hang 三菱銀行 9.26

san-pai-wên-shêng 三百文省 4.23

san-pai-wên-tsu 三百文足 4.23

Seikyū gakusō 青丘學叢 7.20n

sha-chin 沙金 5.21

Shakaikeizaishigaku 社會經濟史學 6.6n

shan-chia 善價 4.21

Shang-fang tsao 上方造 5.11

Shang-hai-shih t'ung-chih-kuan ch'i-k'an 上海市通志館期刊 9.12n

Shang-lin 上林 3.8

shang-pi 上幣 2.5

Shan-hsi p'iao-chuang k'ao-lüeh 山西票莊考畧 9.1n

Shan-hsi p'iao-hao shih 山西票號史 9.1n

Shao-chou 韶州 4.28

sha-pan 沙板 4.7

sha-wei ch'ien 沙尾錢 4.7

shê 社 8.16–8.18, 8.22

Shê-chu 社主 8.22

Shê-hui k'o-hsüeh tsa-chih 社會科學雜誌 4.26n

Shê-hsien hui-kuan lu 歙縣會館錄 10.37

shê-i 社邑 8.16

shêng 省 4.23

shêng-pai 省陌 4.23

shêng-yin-hang 省銀行 9.21

shên-ku 身股 9.9

shê-ssŭ chuan-t'ieh 社司轉帖 8.16

shê-ts'ang 社倉 8.19

Shê-yu 社友 8.22

Shien 史淵 6.3n

Shigaku 史學 4.10n

Shigaku zasshi 史學雜誌 6.6n

shih 石 8.19

Shih-i fa 市易法 10.19

shih-ku 時估 6.36

shih-li pên-ch'ien 食利本錢 10.15

Shih-liao yü shih-hsüeh 史料與史學 7.1n

Shih-p'i-p'an shu 十批判書 2.7n

Shih-san-ching chu-su 十三經注疏 2.2n

Shih-tsung 世宗 6.29

Shih-t'ung 十通 4.2n

Shih-ya 石雅 4.24n

Shina kaheikō 支那貨幣考 4.1n

Shina kaheishi sensōkō 支那貨幣史錢莊考 5.23n

Shina keizai sensho 支那經濟全書 9.7

Shinashi kenkyū 支那史研究 2.14n

Shirin 史林 8.16n

shou 手 2.14

Shou-ch'un 壽春 5.5

shou-kuei 首櫃 8.9

shu 銖 2.22, 3.5–3.13, 3.16, 3.19, 3.30, 3.31, 4.3, 4.11, 5.4

Shuang-chu 雙柱 5.27

Shu-ching 書經 5.4n

Shu-chung kuang-chi 蜀中廣記 6.12n

shu-fang 書放 6.12

shuo-ta-hua, shih-hsiao-ch'ien 說大話使小錢 4.16

Shuo-wên chieh-tzǔ 說文解字 2.12

so 索 2.14

Sogabe Shizuo 曾我部靜雄 6.10n

ssǔ-ch'ao 絲鈔 7.5

Ssǔ-ch'ao ch'ao-pi t'u-lu 四朝鈔幣圖錄 6.27n

ssǔ-Ch'ien-hao 四乾號 9.19

ssǔ-chu 私鑄 4.1, 4.5, 4.9

ssǔ-hang 四行 9.29

ssǔ-hsiao 私銷 4.9

Ssǔ-k'u ch'üan-shu chên-pên ch'u-chi 四庫全書珍本初集 6.12n

ssǔ-kung yin 四工銀 5.28

Ssǔ-ma Ch'ien 司馬遷 10.12

ssǔ-p'iao 司票 7.30

Ssǔ-pu pei-yao 四部備要 7.31n

Ssǔ-pu ts'ung-k'an 四部叢刊 2.5n

ssǔ-ta-Hêng 四大恒 9.20

ssǔ-t'i ch'ien 四體錢 3.23

Sung-t'ung yüan-pao 宋通元寶 3.20, 4.14

Sung-yüan t'ung-pao 宋元通寶 3.20, 3.21

Sun-t'ou 孫頭 5.34

ta-ch'ao 大鈔 6.28

ta-ch'ien 大錢 4.10

Ta-Ch'ing yin-hang 大清銀行 9.28

ta-chin p'u 打金鋪 8.33

Ta-chou 達州 5.14

ta-ch'üan wu-shih 大泉五十 3.10, 3.11

tai 貸 10.6

ta-i-fên 大一分 10.9

T'ai-ho wu-shu 太和五銖 4.2

T'ai-ku 太谷 9.6

T'ai-kung 太公 3.1

T'ai-p'ing hsing-pao 太平興寶 3.25

T'ai-p'ing shan-jên 太平山人 4.26n

tai-pu 代步 8.5

tai-tang 代當 8.5

T'ai-wan yin-hang 臺灣銀行 9.26

Ta-li yin 大禮銀 5.14

Ta-Ming pao-ch'ao 大明寶鈔 7.24

tan 膽 4.28

T'an-chou 潭州 4.28, 5.14

tang 當 8.4, 8.6

Tang Êrh-niang 黨二娘 10.4

T'ang Hsiang-lung 湯象龍 4.26n

T'ang Yü-k'un 唐與崑 4.30n

tang-p'iao 當票 8.7

tang-p'u 當鋪 8.3

tang-shih 當十 4.14

T'ang-tai ching-chi shih 唐代經濟史 6.3n

T'ang-tai ts'ai-chêng shih 唐代財政史 1.8n

tang-tien 當店 8.4

tang-wu 當五 4.14

tan-shui 膽水 4.28

tan-t'ung 膽銅 4.28

tao 刀 2.15

tao 道 9.13

T'ao Hsi-shêng 陶希聖 6.3n

tao-chu 盜鑄 4.5

tao-huan 倒換 7.20

Tao-shêng yin-hang 道勝銀行 9.26

ta-tang 打當 8.8

Ta-t'ung yin-hang 大通銀行 9.26

ta-yang 大洋 5.35

Ta-Ying yin-hang 大英銀行 9.26

ta-yin p'u 打銀鋪 8.33

Tê-Hua yin-hang 德華銀行 9.26

Têng T'ung 鄧通 4.1

tiao 吊 4.15–4.19

t'iao-ch'ao 挑鈔 7.18, 7.22

t'iao-ta ch'ien-chuang 挑打錢莊 9.15

t'iao-tan 挑擔 9.15

t'ieh 帖 8.28

t'ieh-ch'ien 鐵錢 3.30

tien 典 8.4

T'ien Wên-ching 田文鏡 8.35n

T'ien-fu chên-pao 天福鎮寶 3.25

T'ien-hsia chün-kuo li-ping shu 天下郡國利病書 8.13n

T'ien-hsing pao-hui 天興寶會 6.38

T'ien-ming 天命 3.24

tien-tang 典當 8.3

T'ien-ts'ung 天聰 3.24

Tien-t'ung 滇銅 4.29

ti-kuan 敵貫 6.5

ting 錠 5.13, 5.14, 5.20, 5.21, 7.4, 7.7, 7.10, 7.17

Ting Fu-pao 丁福保 2.15n

t'ing-lu chien-mao 停爐減卯 4.30

ti-tang k'u 抵當庫 8.3

Tōa senshi 東亞錢志 1.14n, 2.15n, 5.14

Tōhō gakuhō 東方學報 2.15n

Tōsō hōritsu bunsho no kenkyū 唐宋法律文書の研究 10.2n

Tōsō jidai ni okeru kingin no kenkyū 唐宋時代に於ける金銀の
研究 2.24n

tou-chi 斗級 10.35

Tōyō bunka kenkyū 東洋文化研究 9.2n

Tōyō gakuhō 東洋學報 6.10n

Tōyō rekishi daijiten 東洋歷史大辭典 6.23n

Tōyōshi kenkyū 東洋史研究 4.26n

Ts'ai-chou 蔡州 6.38

tsan-ch'ien hui 攢錢會 8.26

Ts'ao Hsüeh-ch'üan 曹學佺 6.12n

ts'ao-p'ing 漕平 5.23

ts'ao-shu 草書 3.22

Ts'ê-fu yüan-kuei 冊府元龜 2.25n

Tsiang, C. C. 蔣仲川 5.30n

Tso Tsung-t'ang 左宗棠 10.27

Tso Wên-hsiang kung ch'üan-chi 左文襄公全集 7.30n

tso-ch'üan 左券 10.2

ts'o-tao 錯刀 2.21

tsou-kao 奏稿 7.30n

tsu 足 4.23

Ts'ui Shên-yu 崔慎由 5.13

tsung-hang 總行 9.23

tsung-lun 總論 3.4n

Ts'ung-shu chi-ch'êng 叢書集成 10.22n

tsu-pai 足陌 4.22, 4.23

tuan-pai 短陌 4.21

Tuan-wu chin-fêng-yin 端午進奉銀 5.13

tui-ch'ien 對錢 3.22

tui-chin hui 堆金會 8.26

tui-fang 兌房 8.32

tui-pien-chih-p'u 兌便之鋪 8.32

tui-tu 對讀 3.17

T'ung Kuo-t'ai 童國泰 10.24

tung-ch'ien 東錢 4.22

t'ung-ch'ien 銅錢 4.24

t'ung-ch'ü jên 同取人 10.6

Tung-fang hui-li yin-hang 東方匯理銀行 9.26

Tung-fang yin-hang 東方銀行 9.24, 9.26

t'ung-pao 通寶 3.16–3.18

t'ung-tzǔ-êrh 銅子兒 4.16

t'ung-yüan 銅元 3.26, 3.27, 4.16, 7.35

t'un-tang 囤當 8.12

Tu-shih 都市 5.11

tzŭ 子 4.13

tzŭ-ch'ien chia 子錢家 1.15

tzŭ-mo chin 紫磨金 5.21

tzŭ-mu hsiang-ch'üan 子母相權 4.10-4.13

Wang An-shih 王安石 10.19, 10.21

Wang Ching-ju 王靜如 3.24n

Wang Kuo-wei 王國維 3.35n

Wang Ming-yüan 王名元 2.4n

Wang Mang 王莽 1.11, 2.13, 2.21, 3.10-3.14, 10.12, 10.21

Wang Tsung-p'ei 王宗培 8.15n

Wang Yü-ch'üan 王毓銓 2.6n

Wang-tao 王刀 2.20

Wei Chou 韋宙 8.18

Wei Chü-hsien 衛聚賢 9.1n

wei-ch'ao 偽鈔 7.18

Wêng Wên-kung kung jih-chi 翁文恭公日記 9.18n

Wêng T'ung-ho 翁同龢 9.18n

Wên-hsien t'ung-k'ao 文獻通考 4.2n

Wo-t'o ch'ien 斡脫錢 10.20

Wo-t'o chü 斡脫局 10.21

Wo-t'o so 斡脫所 10.21

Wo-t'o tsung-kuan fu 斡脫總管府 10.21

Wu Han 吳晗 7.1n

Wu, Prince of 吳王 4.1

wu-T'ien-hao 五天號 9.19

wu-Yü 五宇 9.18

ya 押 8.4

Yang Chao-yü 楊肇遇 8.8n

Yang Chung-min kung i-pi 楊忠愍公遺筆 10.22n

Yang Hsi-mêng 楊西孟 8.15n

Yang Shih 楊時 10.22

yang-ch'ien 洋錢 5.27

Yang-ch'un pai-hsüeh 陽春白雪 7.20n

yang-kao-êrh-li 羊羔兒利 10.20

yang-t'ung 洋銅 4.29.

Yao Sui 姚燧 2.30n

yao-ch'üan i-shih 幺泉一十 3.11

yao-hui 搖會 8.24

ya-tien 押店 8.4

Yeh-Lü Ch'u-ts'ai 耶律楚材 7.4

Yen 燕 3.3

yen-ch'ao 鹽鈔 6.26

yen-chiao-ch'ao 鹽交鈔 6.26

yen-chiao-yin 鹽交引 6.26

yen-yin 鹽引 6.26

yin 引 6.23

yin 銀 5.1

yin-ch'ai 銀拆 10.29

yin-ch'ao 銀鈔 5.19

yin-chiang 銀匠 5.11

yin-chiang p'u 銀匠鋪 8.30

yin-ch'ien-pu-fu ch'üan-i-ch'ou-tai 因錢不敷權以籌代 2.30

Yin-ching fa-mi 銀經發祕 5.27-5.28n

yin-fei 銀飛 7.33

ying-yang 鷹洋 5.27

Ying-yüan 郢爰 5.5

ying-yün 營運 10.21, 10.31, 10.38

ying-yün hu 營運戶 10.21

yin-hang 銀行 9.23

yin-hang t'uan 銀行團 9.24

yin-hao 銀號 9.12, 9.17

yin-huang 銀荒 4.26n

yin-hui 銀會 6.18

yin-hui-tzŭ 銀會子 6.18

yin-ku 銀股 9.9

yin-lou 銀樓 8.33

yin-lu 銀爐 5.24, 8.33, 8.34

yin-p'iao 銀票 7.29, 7.31

yin-p'u 銀鋪 8.30, 8.33

yin-tzŭ 印子 10.30

yin-tzŭ-ch'ien 印子錢 10.30

yü 宇 9.18–9.20

yüan 爰 (鍰) 5.3–5.5

Yüan Chên 元稹 2.26n

Yüan-tien-chang 元典章 2.30n, 7.18

Yüan-ch'ü hsüan 元曲選 8.25n

yüan-fa 圜法 3.1

Yüan-kuang chên-pao 元光珍寶 6.37

Yüan-kuang chung-pao 元光重寶 6.37

yüan-pao 元寶 1.12, 3.16–3.18, 5.22

yüan-pao ch'ao 元寶鈔 3.18

Yüan-shih Ch'ang-ch'ing chi 元氏長慶集 2.26n

Yüan-shih shih-fan 袁氏世範 10.22

Yüan t'ou 袁頭 5.34

yüan-tsu pu 圜足布 2.17

Yüan-tzŭ-chuang 元字莊 9.15

yü-chia ch'ien 榆莢錢 3.5

yu-ch'üan 右券 10.2

yu-ch'üan êrh-shih 幼泉二十 3.11

Yüeh-man-t'ang jih-chi pu 越縵堂日記補 9.18n

Yü-fêng 宇豐 9.18

Yü-hêng 宇恒 9.18

Yu-Hua yin-hang 友華銀行 9.26

Yu-li yin-hang 有利銀行 9.26

Yung-chêng chu-p'i yü-chih 雍正硃批諭旨 8.13n

Yung-chou 永州 8.18

Yün-wei 云為 10.21

Yün-wei hu 云為戶 10.21

Yü-shêng 宇升 9.18